A to Z 神秘案件

中英双语
第一辑

The Empty Envelope
一个空信封

[美]罗恩·罗伊 著
[美]约翰·史蒂文·格尼 绘　杨琼琼 译

湖南少年儿童出版社
小博集
·长沙·

人物介绍

三人小组的成员，聪明勇敢，喜欢读推理小说，紧急关头总能保持头脑冷静。喜欢在做事之前好好思考！

丁丁

三人小组的成员，活泼机智，喜欢吃好吃的食物，常常有意想不到的点子。

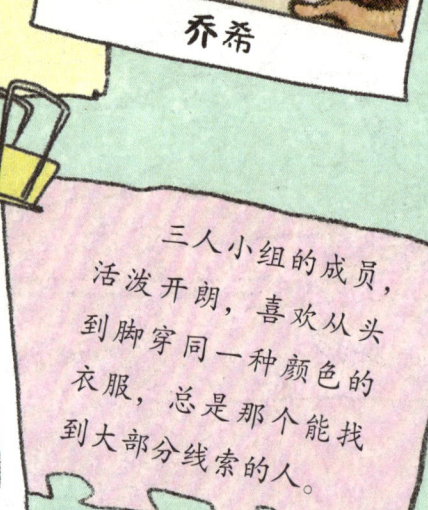

乔希

三人小组的成员，活泼开朗，喜欢从头到脚穿同一种颜色的衣服，总是那个能找到大部分线索的人。

露丝

被寄错的信的主人，专程从科罗拉多州到康涅狄格州来取信。

多丽丝·邓肯

信封上署名的寄信人，因为抄错邮政编码，把信寄到了绿地镇。

欧托·伯德

从家里的旧吸尘器里发现了一张珍稀邮票，后来又把邮票弄丢了。

克莱芒蒂娜·潘特尔

字母 E 代表 enemy，敌人，……

    孩子们透过树篱看过去，看到一个男人和一个女人下了车。那个男人身材矮小，穿着绿色的西服，系着紫色的领带。

    "就是他！"乔希小声说，"之前我看到的在车里的那个人！"

    孩子们看到那个男人和那个女人聊了一会儿，然后一起回到车上，但是并没有开车离开。

    "他们到底要干什么？"乔希问。

    丁丁倒吸了一口气，用手摁住藏在衬衫里的信封。

    "他们在等我。"他说。

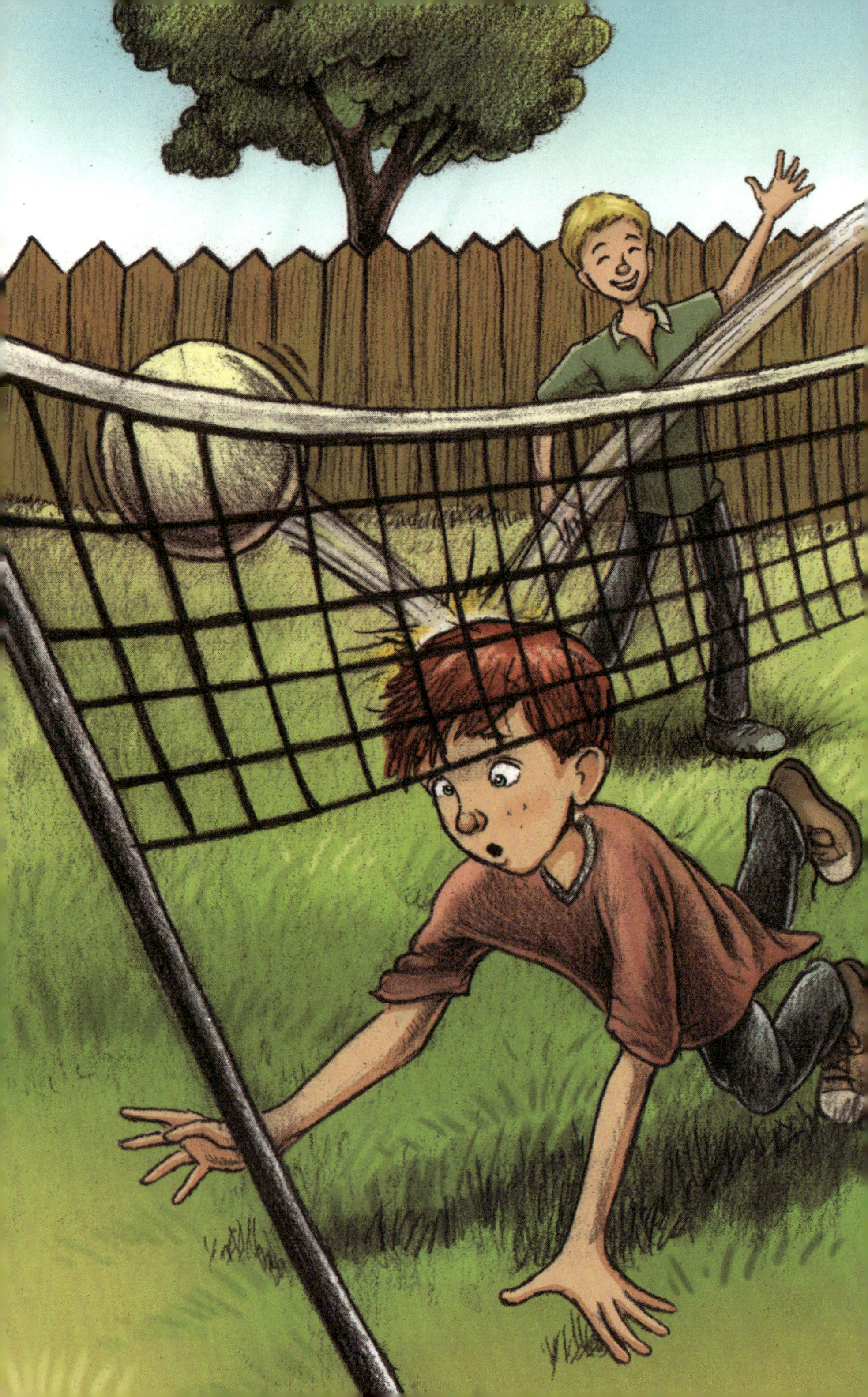

第一章

"我来接!我来接!"乔希在丁丁家的后院边跑边叫,从一边跑到另一边。他用力一跳,没有接住排球,反倒摔了一跤。

丁丁哈哈大笑道:"你来接,你来接,这下接得可真好!"

"干得好,纳特!"露丝大声叫道。纳特是她的弟弟,只有四岁。露丝和他击了一下掌:"你刚才为我们又得了一分。"

纳特的小脸变红了，朝姐姐不好意思地笑了笑。

乔希从地上爬起来，咧着嘴笑道："好吧，我要好好比赛了。从现在开始，看我和丁丁的。"

就在这时，他们听见嘟的一声喇叭响。"鲁比来送信了。"露丝说。

乔希丢下手里的排球，对丁丁说："我想知道，你今天是不是还会收到一个蓝色信封。我真想马上看看那个'妈妈'今天写了些什么。"

丁丁跑到房子前，鲁比在卡车上向他招了招手，然后就开车走了。丁丁打开信箱，把手伸了进去。

他拿出了两张寄给爸爸妈妈的账单和一个寄给他的蓝色信封。

上周，丁丁收到了四个蓝色信封，这是第五个了。每一封信都是寄给CO州绿地镇D.邓肯的，邮政编码为06040。不过，信封里的信却是写给一个叫多丽丝的人的，写信人是多丽丝的妈妈。

丁丁跑回后院，高高挥动手里的信。"又收

一个空信封

到一封。"他说。

"很好,打开信封看看。"乔希说。

丁丁撕开信封口,伸手去取里面的信。

"里面没有信。"他说,"信封是空的。"

露丝朝信封里看了看,问道:"为什么那个'妈妈'要邮寄一个空信封呢?"

丁丁耸了耸肩:"先进屋吧,我想再看看其他信件。"

孩子们走进丁丁家的厨房,操作台上放了一个盖着盖子的盘子。

"我妈妈给我们做了三明治。"丁丁说。

纳特伸手去拿三明治盘子,可是他的姐姐制止了他:"看看你的手!我们先到水槽边洗个手吧,纳特。"

丁丁打开抽屉,取出之前收到的四封信,一一摆放在餐桌上,这些信看起来一模一样。

"我能喝点果汁吗?"没等丁丁回答,乔希就打开了冰箱。

丁丁坐在那儿,一边盯着信封看,一边点了点头。每封信的寄信人都是纽约市布鲁克林

11

区嘉露街 10 号的欧·伯德，邮政编码为 11234。
"我不认识布鲁克林的人，"他说，"更别说什么叫欧·伯德的人了。"

丁丁的目光停留在摆放在中间的一个信封上。"嘿，看这里！"他突然说道，手指指向信封上的地址"CO"，"这难道不是科罗拉多州的缩写吗？"

乔希和露丝一人拿起一个信封。

"是的，你说的没错。"乔希说，"康涅狄格

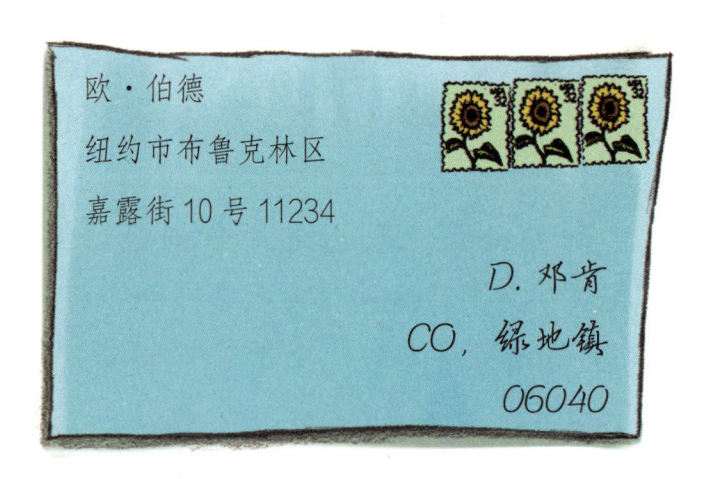

```
欧·伯德
纽约市布鲁克林区
嘉露街 10 号 11234

            D. 邓肯
          CO，绿地镇
            06040
```

一个空信封

州的缩写是 CT，不是 CO。"

丁丁看了看他的朋友们，说："信封上的邮政编码写对了，但是州名写错了。"

"或者是州名写对了，但是邮政编码写错了。"露丝说。

"你这话是什么意思？"乔希问。

"也许这些信是写给科罗拉多州绿地镇的邓肯的。"露丝说，"那个欧·伯德只是写错了邮政编码。"

"我知道怎么弄清楚这件事。"丁丁说。

他走到电话旁，拨通了查询号码，向长途电话接线员询问欧·伯德的电话号码。

"没有这个人？"丁丁说，"好吧，谢谢！"他挂断了电话，说："布鲁克林查询不到欧·伯德这个人。"

"嗯，"乔希拿起一块三明治说，"绿地镇只有你一个人叫邓肯。"

"是康涅狄格州的绿地镇只有我一个人叫邓肯。"丁丁说。

乔希叹了口气："不管了，我们吃东西吧。"

13

A to Z 神秘案件

他们狼吞虎咽地吃完了花生酱和葡萄果酱三明治。

几分钟过后,露丝说:"再看看这几封信,丁丁,也许信里有线索,能告诉我们这些信到底是写给谁的。"

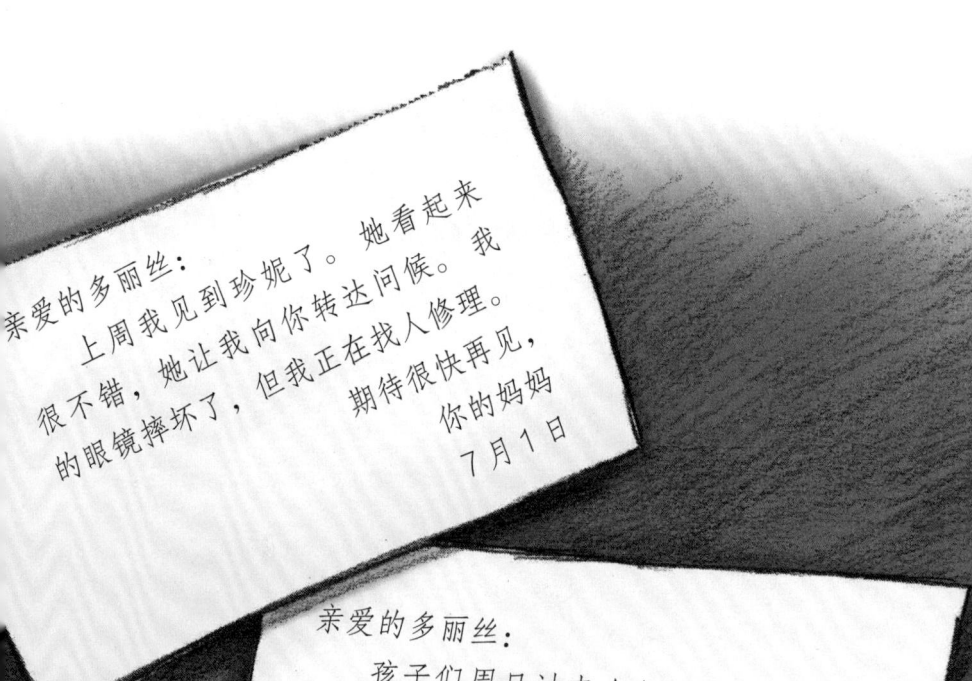

亲爱的多丽丝:

上周我见到珍妮了。她看起来很不错,她让我向你转达问候。我的眼镜摔坏了,但我正在找人修理。期待很快再见,

你的妈妈
7月1日

亲爱的多丽丝:

孩子们周日过来吃午餐了。他们非常可爱。萨莉藏在了活动室里,剩下的时间我们都在找她。

以后再写信给你,
爱你的妈妈
7月3日

一个空信封

丁丁从信封里拿出信,把四封信并排摆放好。

乔希拿起第五个信封,倒过来晃了晃。"也许有人偷了最后一封信。"他神秘地看着丁丁,小声说。

"说不定有间谍盯上了你收到的信,"他说话

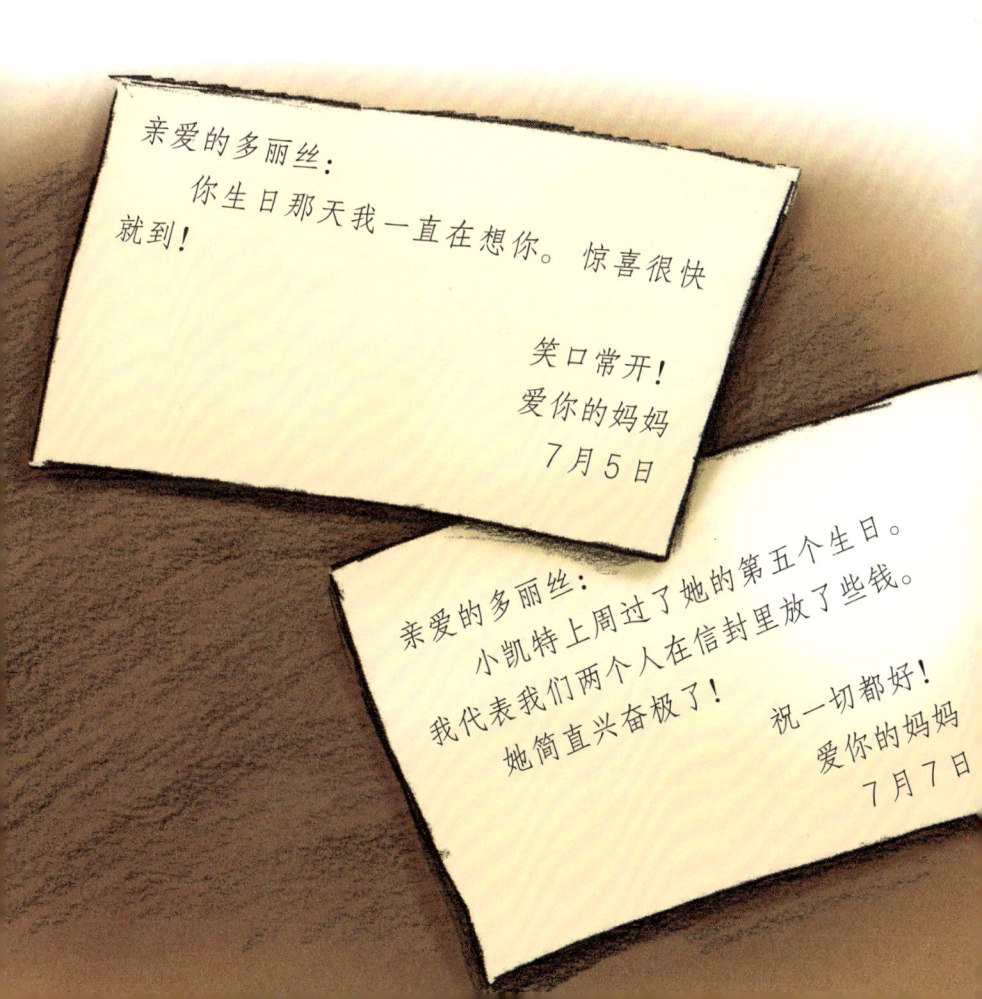

亲爱的多丽丝:
你生日那天我一直在想你。惊喜很快就到!

笑口常开!
爱你的妈妈
7月5日

亲爱的多丽丝:
小凯特上周过了她的第五个生日。我代表我们两个人在信封里放了些钱。她简直兴奋极了!

祝一切都好!
爱你的妈妈
7月7日

时的声音令人毛骨悚然,"也许他们是从海王星过来绑架人类的外星人……"

就在这时,电话响了。

第二章

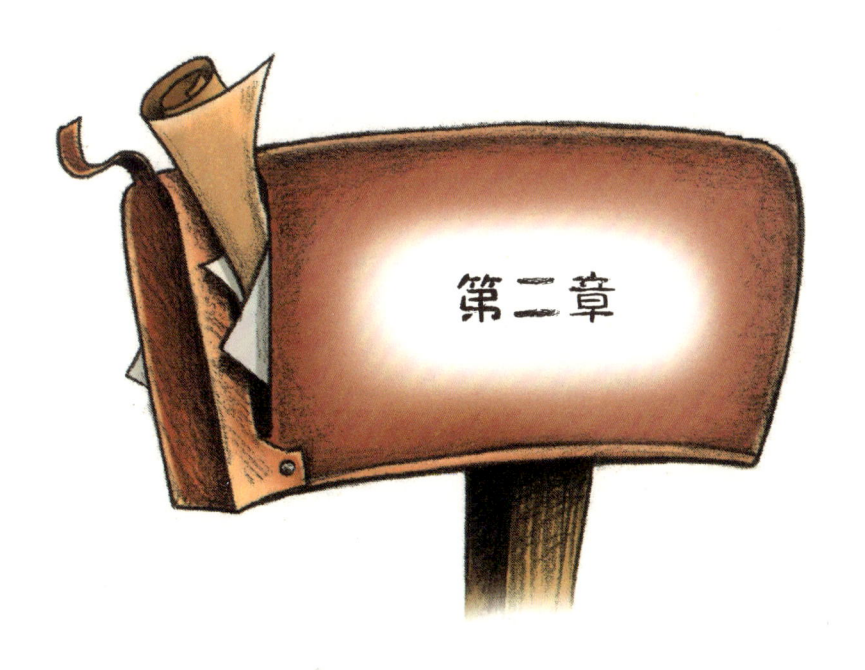

丁丁接听了电话。

"请问是 D. 邓肯吗?"一个女人问。

"我是唐纳德·邓肯,"丁丁回答道,"但我的朋友们都叫我丁丁。"

"好的,丁丁。"那个女人说,"我是科罗拉多州的多丽丝·邓肯,我想你可能收到了一些写给我的信。"

丁丁捂住电话话筒,转身看向乔希和露丝。"是科罗拉多州的一位女士,打电话来要那些信。"他小声说着,兴奋不已。

A to Z 神秘案件

"你好！你在听电话吗？"那个女人问，"别挂断电话！"

丁丁重新对着电话话筒说："嗯……我这周收到了五个蓝色信封。"

"是的，那些信都是写给我的，它们非常重要。"多丽丝·邓肯说，"你什么时候能把这些信还给我？"

丁丁看了一眼厨房。"这些信现在就放在我家的桌子上，"他对多丽丝·邓肯说，"你是想要我把这些信邮寄给你吗？"

"不用！"那个女人厉声说，"不要邮寄给我，我现在就在香格里拉酒店。怎么能找到你？"

"嗯，我想你可以来我家找我。"丁丁说。丁丁告诉那个女人如何到林荫街22号，然后就挂断了电话。

"怎么回事？"露丝问。

丁丁再次坐回到桌旁："是多丽丝·邓肯打来的电话，这些信都是写给她的，她马上就来这里取信。"

"从科罗拉多州来这里？"乔希问。

18

一个空信封

"不,她现在在香格里拉酒店,几分钟后就会到这里。"

"她在康涅狄格州吗?"露丝说,"那也太奇怪了。"

丁丁点了点头:"是啊,还有,她的声音听起来很生气,就像我故意拿了她的信似的。"

"这也太差劲了。"乔希打着哈欠说,"有人把信错寄给了你,现在又有个女人要把这些信取回去。"乔希站起身,伸了个懒腰,说:"我们继续打排球吧。"

丁丁把信重新装回信封,然后将它们放在了装盐的瓶子和装胡椒的瓶子之间。

露丝戳了戳这些信封:"这个女人大老远跑到康涅狄格州来只为拿她妈妈写给她的信,你们有没有觉得这很奇怪?"

"也许她到达这里的时候,丁丁可以去问问她。"乔希说,"拜托,我们现在能去打排球了吗?"

露丝站起身。"这些信为什么那么重要呢?"她往外走时,疑惑地问。

十分钟后,丁丁听到有人和他打招呼:"你好

19

A to Z 神秘案件

啊,年轻人!"

丁丁跑到院子一侧,看到一个高个子女人从人行道向他走来,于是他跑过去迎接她。

"您好!您是邓肯太太吗?"

那个女人高高地立在丁丁面前:"我是邓肯女士,你是丁丁吗?"

为了看清楚这个女人的脸,丁丁不得不往后仰着头。她的头发是黑色的,深色的眼睛有点斜视。她那只硕大强壮的手里紧紧抓着一个小包。

"好吧,你是不是那个和我通过电话的男孩?"那个女人质问。

丁丁倒吸了一口气,说:"是的,女士,我这就去拿信给您。"

"谢谢!"那个女人说,忽然间,她的语气变得友好起来,"那些信是我妈妈贝西·邓肯寄给我的。她上个月去世了,那些是她写给我的最后几封信。"

丁丁向厨房的餐桌走去,准备取信。但是,那些信不见了!

丁丁在厨房里到处找,操作台上没有,冰箱

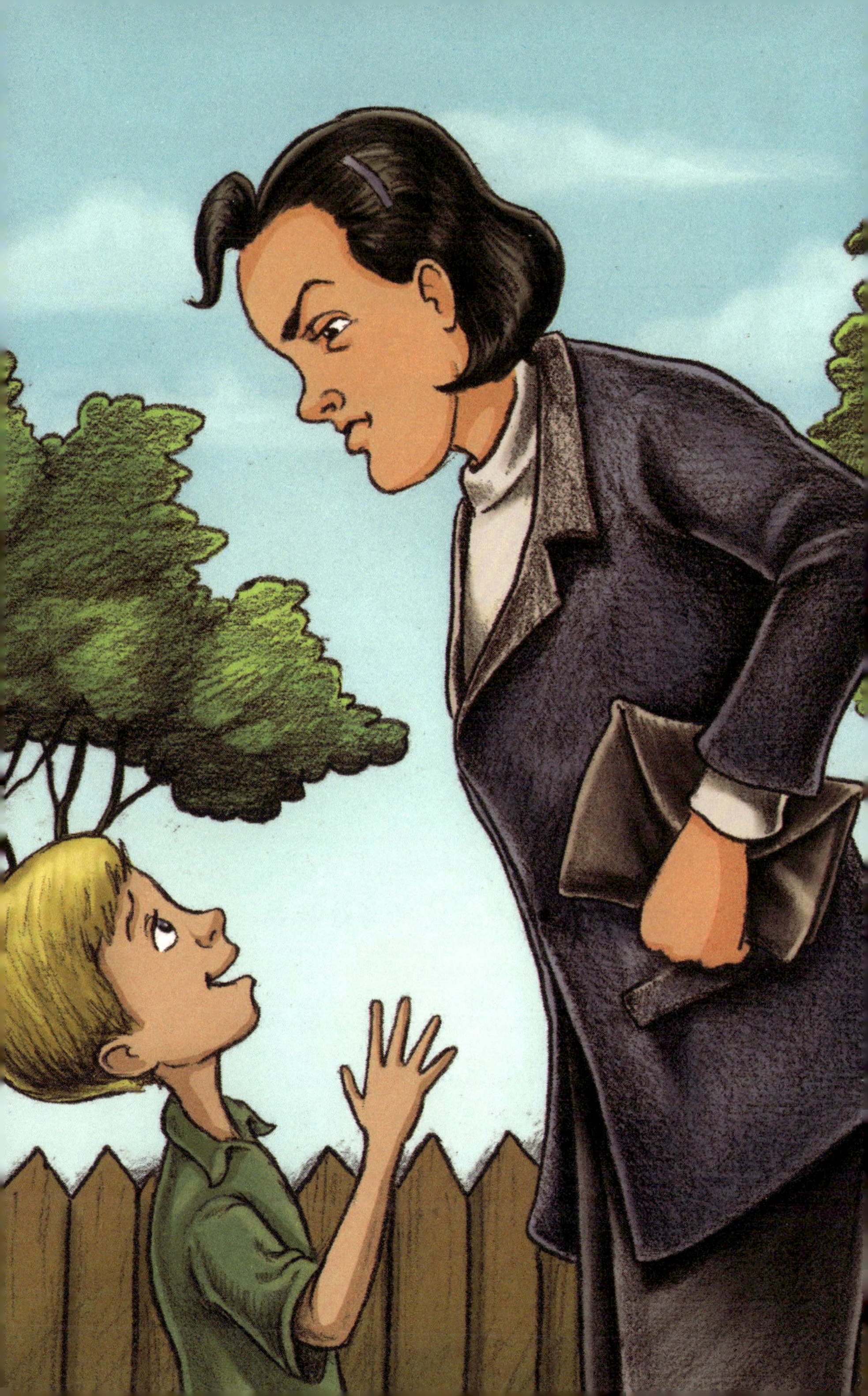

上没有，炉子上也没有。

丁丁在餐桌下的地板上找，只看到了吃午餐时掉下的面包屑，根本没有看到蓝色信封。

"怎么啦？"露丝问。她和乔希正透过厨房后面的纱窗门往里看。

"我找不到那些信了！"丁丁对他的两个朋友说，"吃完午餐后，我不是把它们放在桌子上了吗？"

露丝推开门走了进来："我想你是把它们放在桌子上了。"

露丝看了看烤面包机后面，咖啡机后面，还有微波炉后面。

"帮我们找找，乔希。"丁丁说，"那位女士在等着呢！那些信是她妈妈写给她的，她妈妈上个月去世了。"

乔希走了进来，大家一起在厨房里找那几封信，那些信竟然消失得无影无踪。

"我想我最好把这件事告诉那位女士。"丁丁咕哝着，摇了摇头，"我确定我把信放在桌子上了。"

一个空信封

丁丁穿过客厅,打开前门,多丽丝·邓肯还站在原来的地方没动。

丁丁咽了口唾沫,难过地说:"我……呃,真的很抱歉,我找不到那些信了。"

那个女人俯身瞪着他,问道:"你什么意思?我给你打电话的时候,你说那些信在你这儿,现在它们在哪儿?"

丁丁觉得自己的脸红了。"我不知道。"他小声地说,"刚才它们还在厨房的餐桌上,但是现在却不见了。我的朋友们也帮我找了。"

这个女人的目光越过丁丁,往他身后看。她那神情就像要一把推开丁丁,自己去房子里搜寻一番。

"我妈妈回来以后,我会让她帮我找找。"丁丁说,"您晚点再过来,好吗?"

多丽丝·邓肯用手指在包上敲了敲,说:"我六点整再过来。年轻人,希望到时候我能拿到我的信。"

"别担心,我们会找到信的。"丁丁向她保证,"我妈妈什么都能找到,她是个非常爱收拾

23

东西的狂人。"

这个女人吸了吸鼻子,然后迈着重重的步子从人行道上往街道那边走去。

丁丁看着她离开,然后转身撞上了乔希。

"我要告诉你妈妈,你说她是个非常爱收拾东西的狂人。"乔希咧着嘴笑道。

"偷听别人讲话是不礼貌的,乔希。"丁丁说完就回厨房去了。

"大家看看这个。"露丝指着餐桌上留下的紫色手印说,"我记得我擦过餐桌了。"

乔希弯腰看了看,然后闻了闻那个紫色手印:"是葡萄果酱的味道。"

露丝笑着说:"我想我知道是谁拿走了那些信。"

第三章

丁丁、乔希和露丝一起来到露丝家。他们看到纳特在客厅看电视,手上和嘴上都是紫色的果酱。

"纳特,你拿了丁丁的信吗?"露丝问。

纳特用他那蓝色的大眼睛看着姐姐露丝,摇了摇头,说:"没拿。"

露丝看了丁丁和乔希一眼,转了转眼珠,说:"好吧。那么,到底是谁拿走了信呢?我们看到桌子上有沾了葡萄果酱的你的手指印。"

纳特把手藏到T恤衫下面。"是史泰吉拿了

信。"他小声说。

丁丁蹲在纳特旁边，问道："史泰吉把信放到哪里了呢？"

纳特耸了耸肩，眼睛还盯着电视里正在跳舞的两只恐龙。

"史泰吉到底是谁？"乔希问。

"是纳特最喜欢的恐龙。"说着，露丝把电视关了，"纳特，丁丁真的很需要那些信，你能带我们去看看史泰吉放信的地方吗？"

纳特深深地叹了一口气，站起身走进厨房。大家都跟在他后面。

纳特打开冰箱门，冰箱里有一碗草莓果冻，果冻旁边的架子上放着一个剑龙毛绒玩具。

史泰吉的嘴巴里有五个蓝色信封。

乔希哈哈大笑："哟，纳特，你难道不知道恐龙怕冷吗？"

纳特把史泰吉从架子上拿下来，关上了冰箱门。"史泰吉在扮演邮递员，外面太热了。"纳特说。

露丝把信递给丁丁，对纳特说："未经别人的

一个空信封

允许就把东西拿走,这很不好。"

"没事了,纳特。"丁丁一边说,一边检查信封上是否有紫色污渍。他希望多丽丝·邓肯拿到这些信时,它们是完美的。

丁丁发现信封上有一些葡萄果酱留下的污渍,就用自己的裤子擦了擦。他接着检查信封上的紫色污渍时,又一次注意到了寄信人的地址。

"真奇怪!"丁丁说。

丁丁给乔希和露丝看寄信人的地址:"多丽丝·邓肯的妈妈叫贝西·邓肯,可是为什么信件是一个叫欧·伯德的人寄的呢?"

"或许欧·伯德只是在贝西·邓肯去世后帮她邮寄信的人。"乔希说。

丁丁把信封放在餐桌上摆成一排,然后,他把里面的信抽出来放在信封旁边。

"可是,这又是怎么回事?"丁丁说,"这些信上的日期都是上周,但多丽丝·邓肯对我说她妈妈上个月去世了。"

"我给大家倒点牛奶怎么样?"乔希问。

"去吧!"露丝边说边拿起那个空信封,"谁会给自己的女儿寄个空信封呢?"

丁丁点了点头。"这根本说不通,"他说,"除非这些信不是她妈妈写给她的。"

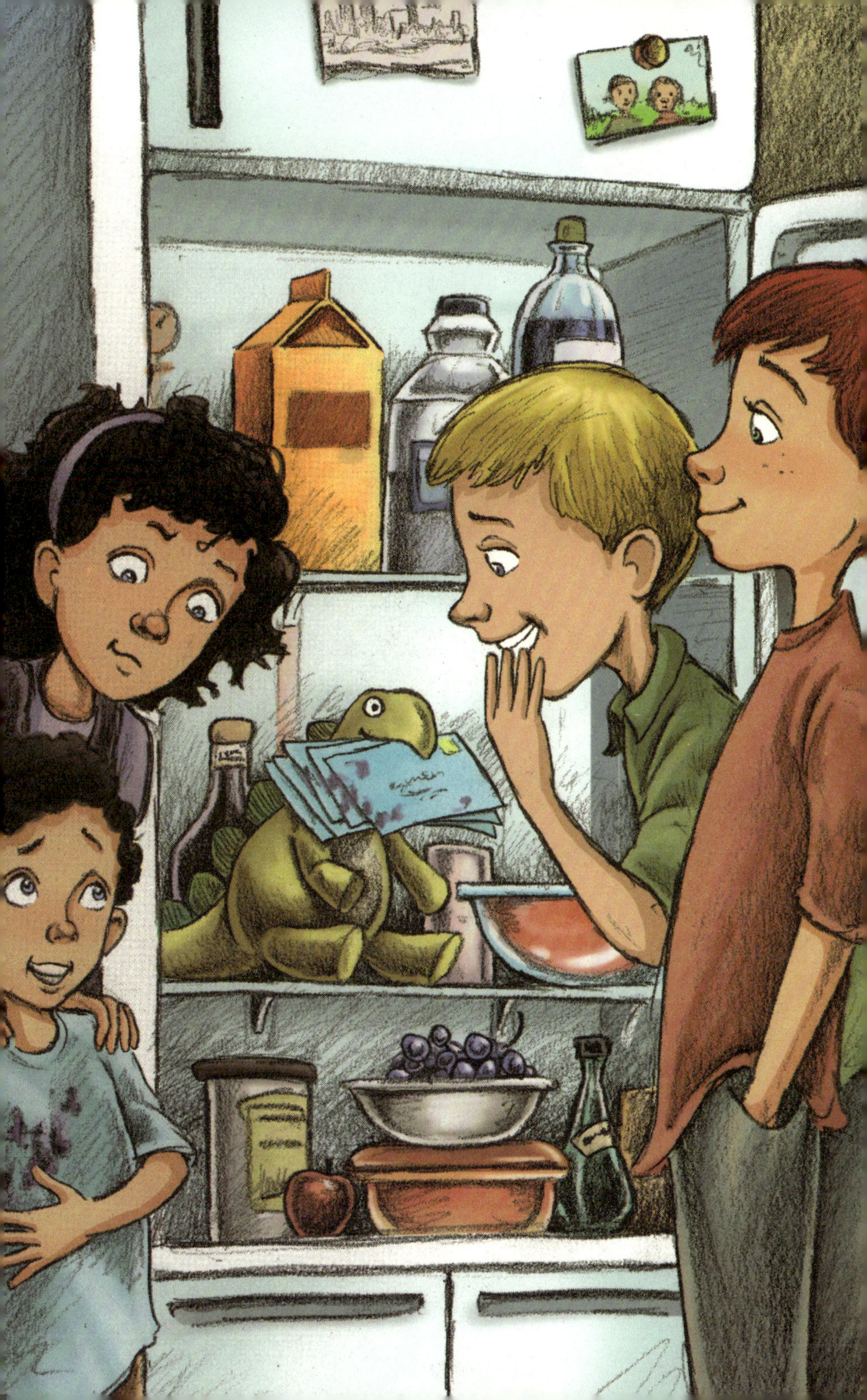

"但是多丽丝为什么要给我们讲一个那样的故事呢？"露丝疑惑地问道。

乔希拿起其中一封信，快速地看了起来。然后，他小心翼翼地倒了一小滴牛奶在信纸上。

"你在干什么！"丁丁大叫，"多丽丝·邓肯不会放过我的！"

"等等！"乔希用手指把那滴牛奶涂抹开，"我看过一本间谍漫画，上面说，如果把牛奶涂抹在隐形墨水写的文字上，那些文字就能显现出来。"乔希说，"也许这些信里有什么秘密信息。"

他们一起俯身看着那张信纸，信纸上没有隐形的文字，反倒多了湿漉漉、黏糊糊的牛奶渍。

"真是谢谢了，乔希！"丁丁说，"你就等着看多丽丝·邓肯看到信后会怎么样吧！"

露丝用一张纸巾擦了擦信纸。"不用担心，它会干的。"她边说边在空中甩了甩信纸，然后把它高举到阳光照射的窗口。

"最好会干！"丁丁说着，对乔希露出一副"否则，你就死定了"的表情。

"伙伴们，快看这个！"露丝说，"这张信纸上

一个空信封

有两个小孔，这两个小孔正好穿过字母H和D。"

乔希拿起另外一封信，把信放在露丝高举着的信的旁边。"这封信上也有一个孔！"他说，"字母J上有一个很小的孔。"

丁丁急忙跳了起来，看着信纸上的小孔，然后，他盯着乔希和露丝说："也许信里真的有秘密信息！"

第四章

孩子们一起检查了另外两封信,他们发现字母O、F和E上也有小孔。

"字母H、D、J、O、F和E上都有小孔。"丁丁边说边在便笺簿上写下这些字母。

"也许这些字母可以拼出什么秘密信息。"露丝说,"我们试试用这些字母拼单词吧。"她把便笺簿拿了过来。

"我拼的单词有hoe、joe、doe和fed。"片刻过后,露丝说。

"我拼出了of、Ed、oh和he。"丁丁说。

一个空信封

"这些单词没有任何意义。"乔希说,"也许每个字母代表一个单词,你们知道的,就像SCUBA这个单词。"

丁丁和露丝都盯着乔希看。

"你们知道SCUBA吧?由S、C、U、B、A这几个字母组成。这些字母代表self-contained underwater breathing apparatus,意思是'自持式水下呼吸器'。"

丁丁咧嘴笑道:"乔希,你怎么看起来那么笨,实际上却那么聪明呢?"

乔希也咧嘴笑着对丁丁说:"你怎么看起来那么笨,而实际上也那么笨呢?"

"各位,别瞎闹了!"露丝说,"我们来弄明白这些字母到底是什么意思吧。"

孩子们花了十分钟的时间猜字母J、H、D、O、F和E想要传递什么信息。

"我放弃!"最后丁丁说。

"等等!"乔希说,"也许那个'妈妈'已经告诉我们秘密信息了。"乔希拿起其中一封信仔细地看了看那些小孔。"你们看!"他说,"这个

A to Z 神秘案件

孔在'envelope（信封）'这个单词的第一个字母 E 上，也许'信封'就是秘密信息的一个单词。"

丁丁和露丝按收信日期的先后顺序将信摆放好，然后再看那些小孔旁边的单词。

丁丁写下了六个单词：Jenny（珍妮）、hid（藏）、den（洞）、on（在上面）、fifth（第五）和

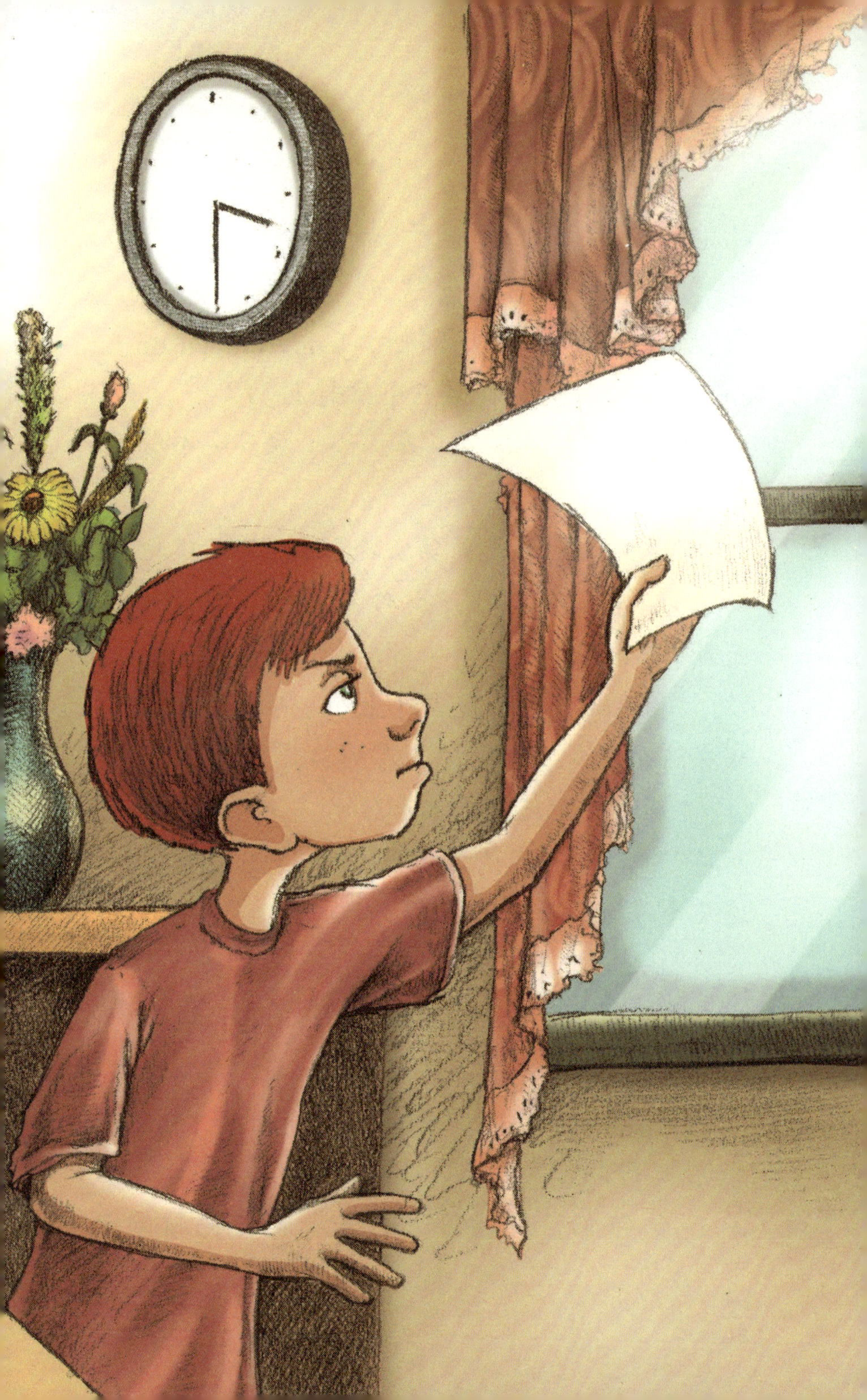

envelope（信封）。

露丝开始大声读这几个单词，然后，她突然咧嘴笑了："大家听，Jenny hidden on fifth envelope.（珍妮藏在第五个信封上。）"

"妙极了！"乔希说着，给了露丝一个赞赏的笑容。

"今天收到的就是第五个信封，"丁丁把信高高举起，问道，"可是，珍妮是谁呢，或者说，是什么呢？"

"信上说珍妮在信封上。"乔希说，"可是，我在这个信封上看到的只有邮票。"

"别忘了，还有墨水和胶水。"丁丁说。

"为什么不试试在地址里找 J、E、N、N、Y 这几个字母呢？"露丝说。

"地址里有字母 E、N、N、Y，"过了一会儿，乔希说，"但是没有字母 J。"

"只能查看邮票了。"丁丁说。这封信的邮票上印着大大的黄色向日葵。"邮票上没有 Jenny（珍妮）。"丁丁说。

"伙伴们，快看！"露丝拿着其他信封说，

一个空信封

"前面四封信的信封上只贴了一张邮票,可是今天收到的这封信的信封上却贴了三张邮票。"

"你说得没错!"丁丁说,"我也觉得奇怪。"他用手指摸了摸那三张向日葵邮票。"我觉得邮票下面有东西!"他说。

丁丁举起信封对着窗户。"这些邮票下面藏了黑黑的东西。"他说,"我能看到那个东西的轮廓!"

第五章

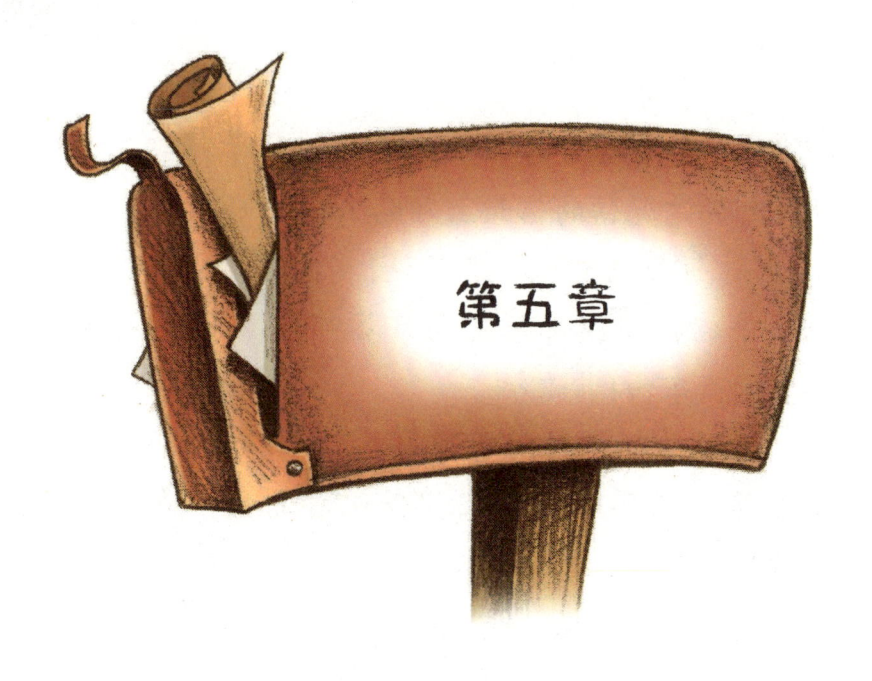

"我去烧点开水。"露丝说,"我爷爷以前集邮,他给我看过怎么用蒸汽使信封上的邮票脱落下来。"

露丝倒了些水到茶壶里,把茶壶放在炉子上,然后把炉子点着了。

大家坐下来盯着茶壶看。

"肯定要很长时间才能烧开。"丁丁咕哝着,用手指尖摸了摸那几张向日葵邮票。

突然,蒸汽从开始咕嘟的茶壶里冒了出来,丁丁把空信封递给露丝。

一个空信封

露丝把信封拿起来,放到茶壶嘴上方,让邮票正对着茶壶嘴。

几秒钟后,邮票变得潮湿,开始一点点从信封上脱落。

"这太酷了!"乔希说,"我感觉自己就像个间谍!"

露丝关了炉子,用牙签的尖端取下信封上的三张向日葵邮票。

三张邮票下面藏着一张更小的邮票,邮票外面包着一层玻璃纸。这张邮票是蓝色的,正中央是一架老式飞机的图片,飞机正在飞行,不过是倒着飞行的。

丁丁撕掉了玻璃纸。"这是一张旧邮票。"他说。

乔希用手指戳了一下那张邮票。"这破邮票印错了。"他咕哝着,"一张飞机印颠倒了的邮票有什么了不起的?"

露丝看了看那张邮票。"也许这张邮票很值钱。"她说,"我爷爷就有一张价值两百美元的邮票。"

A to Z 神秘案件

"不知道多丽丝·邓肯是否知道这张邮票在这个信封上。"丁丁说。

大家你看看我,我看看你,然后又盯着那张小小的蓝色邮票看。

"我们应该去图书馆看看有关邮票的书。"最

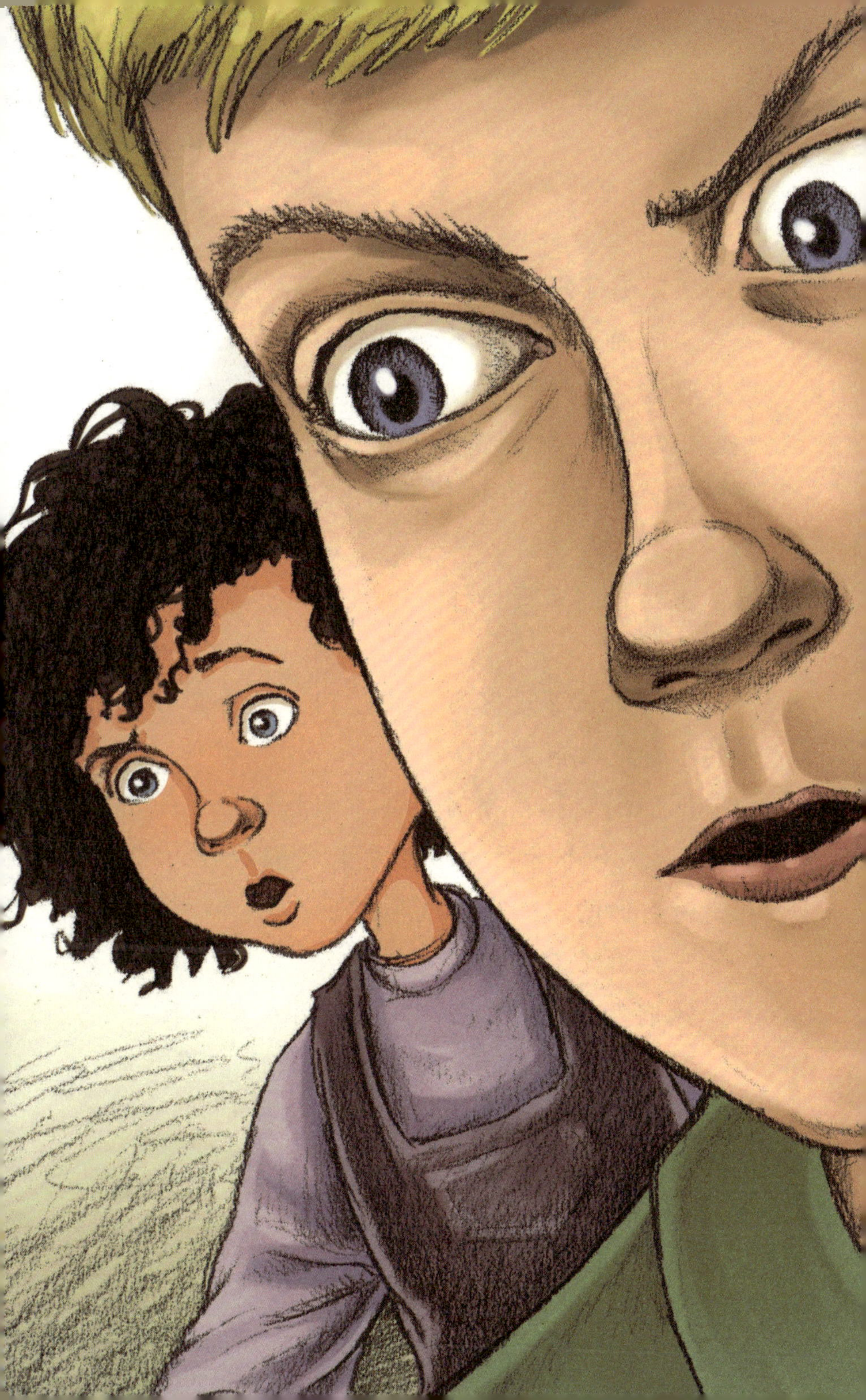

后，露丝说。

丁丁看了一眼厨房的挂钟，说："我们最好快一点，多丽丝·邓肯不到一个小时后就会回到这里来取信。"

丁丁迅速把邮票放进空信封，然后把五个信封都塞到自己的衬衫下面。"好了，我们出发吧。"他说。

露丝走到客厅楼梯口大喊道："妈妈，我去图书馆了！"

他们匆忙穿过客厅，出了门，沿着露丝家前面的人行道往前走。

他们刚到林荫街时，乔希用胳膊撞了一下丁丁。"看，有个奇怪的人在看着我们。"他指着停在街道对面的一辆黑色汽车说。

露丝看了看："什么人？"

他们都朝那边看去，没看到有人在车里。

"快点。"丁丁说，"我们没有时间了。"

孩子们一路跑着去图书馆，当他们冲到图书馆前面的台阶上时，都累得气喘吁吁。

他们突然冲进大门，迈克尔罗伊太太抬头看

一个空信封

着他们，说道："慢一点，孩子们！天哪，你们的脸红得像甜菜。"

"您好，迈克尔罗伊太太！"露丝喘着气说，"您能给我们找一本有关邮票的书吗？"

"你要有关哪种邮票的书呢，露丝？美国的？还是其他国家的？我们这儿有很多有关邮票的书，亲爱的。"

"您这儿有没有哪本书讲到印着颠倒着飞行的飞机的邮票？"丁丁问。

迈克尔罗伊太太笑着说："你是说颠倒邮票吗？也就是不小心印刷反了的邮票。"

她走到一个架子前，拿来一本大书。"你们应该能在这本书里找到你们要找的邮票。"迈克尔罗伊太太说。

"非常感谢您！"丁丁说。

丁丁把书拿到角落里的一张桌子上，坐了下来。他看了看周围，然后从衬衫下面拿出那些信。

他小心翼翼地拿出那张蓝色邮票，将它放到桌子上。

"这里有太多颠倒邮票了！"乔希一边快速翻

阅读

一个空信封

着书页，一边说，"我们怎么才能找到要找的邮票呢？"

"看索引。"丁丁说，"在 Jenny（珍妮）条目下面找。"

乔希翻到书后的索引，在字母 J 的区域里用手指一个一个地指着找。"没有 Jenny（珍妮）这一条。"他说。

"再试试 Airplane（飞机）条目。"露丝说。

"好主意！"乔希往前翻了几页，在字母 A 的索引区域里找到了飞机所在的那一页，接着翻到了第 329 页。

就在那一页，那张蓝色邮票的图片被找到了。

邮票的图片下面是那架飞机的图片，比邮票上的印得更大些。飞机的图片下面写着"单引擎飞机——柯蒂斯·珍妮"。

"嘿！"乔希说，"珍妮就是这架飞机！"

孩子们静静地阅读着有关这张邮票的文字介绍。

"噢，天哪！"露丝大叫。

迈克尔罗伊太太用铅笔在桌子上敲了敲。"露

A to Z 神秘案件

丝,请安静!"她说。

丁丁拿起那张小小的珍妮邮票,他的手指都在颤抖。

"这张邮票价值五万美元!"丁丁小声说。

第六章

"五……五万……我的天哪!"乔希尖叫起来。

大家盯着那张小小的蓝色邮票。过了一会儿,丁丁才把那张邮票塞回信封并放回口袋。

"难怪多丽丝·邓肯要从那么远的地方来康涅狄格州!"露丝说。

丁丁点了点头:"没错,她一直都想要回这张邮票。我觉得她讲的那个有关她妈妈的故事有点可疑。"

乔希合上那本关于邮票的大书:"好了,我们还是得把邮票还给她。"

丁丁和露丝互相看了看对方。

"不是吗?"乔希问

"我想……"丁丁说。

"你想,是什么意思?"乔希说,"邮票是她的,丁丁,邮票在她的信封上,不管这些信是谁寄给她的。"

"可是为什么寄信的人要把这张邮票藏起来呢?"丁丁问,"为什么要编造关于多丽丝妈妈的故事?还假装写那几封信呢?除非……"

"除非什么?"乔希问。

丁丁看着乔希和露丝:"除非这张邮票是偷来的……"

"对!"露丝说,"这张邮票值这么多钱,很有可能是欧·伯德偷来的。然后,他或她得想办法把这张邮票给多丽丝,所以,他们就虚构了多丽丝的妈妈给她写信的故事。"

乔希只是盯着他们俩看。"你们都疯了。"最后他说,"另外,我们也不能肯定。"

露丝跳起来说:"欧·伯德是从纽约寄的信,对吧?也许那就是他偷邮票的地方。"

一个空信封

露丝急忙跑到迈克尔罗伊太太的桌子旁,快速地和她聊了几句,然后又跑了回来。

"发生什么事了?"丁丁问。

"迈克尔罗伊太太会给我们找来前几周的《纽约时报》。"露丝说,"我们可以看看里面有没有关于丢失的邮票的消息。"

丁丁看了看挂钟:"五点十五分,再过四十五分钟,多丽丝·邓肯就要去我家找我了。"

迈克尔罗伊太太走过来,把一大堆《纽约时报》放在了他们的桌子上:"这些是最近的《纽约时报》。孩子们,祝你们好运!"

乔希盯着堆得像小山一样的报纸说:"天哪!我们要花一个晚上才能看完这些报纸。"

"我们没有一个晚上的时间。"丁丁一边伸手拿报纸,一边说,"开始看报纸吧!"

丁丁、乔希和露丝每个人拿了一沓报纸。他们把不需要看的版面放在一边,比如,体育、房地产和娱乐新闻。

他们翻阅了差不多半个小时的报纸。

迈克尔罗伊太太桌子上方的挂钟嘀嗒嘀嗒地

A to Z 神秘案件

响着,时间一分一秒地过去了。

"我的眼睛都看花了。"乔希说,"纽约被偷的东西可真多,有个人竟然偷走了动物园的一只黑猩猩。"

丁丁因为低头趴在桌面上看报纸,看得背部疼痛。他的头也很疼,手指还因为沾到好多油墨,变成灰黑色的了。

就在这个时候,他找到了关于丢失的邮票的消息。

一个空信封

"找到了!"丁丁说。他指着一个大标题读了起来。

老人巨额财富得而复失

6月20日,73岁的克莱芒蒂娜·潘特尔女士,在短暂地当了一段时间的富翁后,现在又变成了穷人。潘特尔女士在清理吸尘器时,在灰尘里发现了一枚珍稀邮票。但随后,在她的房间里,这枚价值超过五万美元的邮票被盗。纽约市警方正在就此事展开调查。

乔希倒吸了一口气。"你说得对,丁丁。"他小声说,"你不能把邮票交给多丽丝·邓肯。"

迈克尔罗伊太太走到他们的桌子边,说:"我马上要下班了。"

丁丁回头看了看挂钟，五点四十八分！"各位，我们还有十二分钟。多丽丝·邓肯就要去我家了。"

他们谢过迈克尔罗伊太太，把报纸堆在一起，匆忙走出了图书馆。

走在图书馆门前的台阶上时，丁丁说："也许我们应该把多丽丝·邓肯的事情告诉法伦警官。"

"可是我们还没办法证明是她干了坏事。"乔希说。

"乔希说得对，丁丁。"露丝说，"多丽丝·邓肯从来没有拿到那些信或者那张邮票，如果你对法伦警官说她和欧·伯德偷了邮票，他们会让我们提供证据。"

"但是我该怎么办呢？"丁丁问，"快六点了！我该怎么对多丽丝·邓肯说呢？"

孩子们开始朝林荫街走去。

"我有个想法！"露丝说，"我们为什么不把向日葵邮票重新粘到空信封上，然后把那五封信都交给多丽丝·邓肯呢？她可能会把信带到酒店再看。然后，我们就跑回来把珍妮邮票交给法伦

一个空信封

警官,并给他讲述整件事的经过。"

"但是,那样做怎么证明她犯法了呢?"丁丁问。

"因为到时候那几封信在她手里啊!"乔希说。

露丝点了点头:"等法伦警官从多丽丝那里拿到信,读到信中隐藏的信息后,他就会知道是她和欧·伯德偷了那张邮票。"

丁丁笑着说:"没错,到那时,我们就可以告诉法伦警官我们刚才在报纸上看到的消息。好,就这样做,我们走吧!"

他们匆匆走下图书馆台阶时,丁丁看到一辆黑色汽车从马路边开走了。

"嘿,乔希,这辆车和你看到的停在我们街道上的那辆车是同一辆车吗?"丁丁问。

"是的,开车的还是那个看起来很奇怪的人!"乔希说。

"乔希,那个时候没有人在车上。"露丝说。

"也许你朝那里看的时候,他藏起来了。"乔希说,"但是,我确定,我看到了驾驶座上有人。"

53

"不管是谁,我们都得走了。"丁丁说,"马上就要到六点钟了。"

孩子们沿着主街一直往前跑。

他们走了一条捷径,先穿过中心公园,随后跑过玫瑰园。

到达林荫街时,他们都累得上气不接下气了。

离丁丁家还有几栋房子的距离时,乔希突然一把抓住丁丁和露丝的手臂,拽着他们蹲下,藏到了阿卢比茨基小姐家门前的树篱后面。

"怎么啦?"丁丁问。

"那辆车又停到你家门前了!"乔希说。

孩子们透过树篱看过去,看到一个男人和一个女人下了车。丁丁认出了多丽丝·邓肯。那个男人身材矮小,穿着绿色的西服,系着紫色的领带。

"就是他!"乔希小声说,"之前我看到的在车里的那个人!"

孩子们看到多丽丝和那个男人聊了一会儿,然后重新回到车上,但是并没有开车离开。

"他们到底要干什么?"乔希问。

一个空信封

　　丁丁倒吸了一口气,用手摁住藏在衬衫里的信封,那可是装着价值五万美元邮票的信封啊!
　　"他们在等我。"他说。

第七章

"我们怎么办？"露丝问，"那个人看起来是个坏人。"

"也许我们应该把信交给他们。"乔希说。

"我们不能那样做！"丁丁说，"那三张向日葵邮票还在露丝家呢！他们一定会知道我们发现了那张被盗的邮票。"

"这样我们就不能回家了。"露丝说，"他们可能会把我们抓走，然后搜我们的身，最后会发现那张邮票藏在丁丁身上。"

"我们从后院穿过去，到我家去吧。"乔希

一个空信封

说,"我们可以打电话给法伦警官,告诉他有人在跟踪我们。"

"好主意!"丁丁说,"我们不能就这样一直待在这里。"

孩子们手脚并用地从阿卢比茨基小姐家的草坪爬过。突然,她家的狗朝他们吠叫起来。

丁丁回头看了一眼那辆车,驾驶室的门一下子打开了,那个穿绿色西服的男人下了车,朝他们又喊又叫。

"我们快跑!"乔希大叫道。他们跳了起来,从阿卢比茨基小姐家的后院跑了。

那个男人追在他们后面,撞进了阿卢比茨基小姐家的树篱。

"他追上来了!"丁丁大叫,"再跑快一点!"

孩子们飞快跑过老鹰巷,一头扎进小树林,藏到了茂密的灌木丛后,想要喘气。

那个男人在树林边停了下来,孩子们看见他弯下腰,大口喘着粗气。

"快点跑!"乔希小声说。他们才刚开始继续跑,那个男人就冲进树林里继续追他们。

A to Z 神秘案件

　　他们跑得比那个男人快，片刻之后，他们穿过了乔希家的院子。

　　"跑到谷仓里去，爬上阁楼！"乔希大叫。

　　"可是我们会被困在那儿的！"丁丁说。

　　"快进去！"乔希说，"我有办法！"

　　三个孩子用最快的速度跑到谷仓里，丁丁和露丝踩着乔希的绳梯爬进了阁楼。

一个空信封

　　丁丁趴在阁楼上往下看，看到乔希把谷仓的后门打开，不过他没有出去，而是跳进了一堆干草里。

　　丁丁简直不敢相信自己的眼睛！"乔希就藏在那里！"丁丁对露丝说。

　　"快！把绳梯拉上来！"露丝小声说。

　　丁丁抓住那条绳梯把它收到了阁楼上。

　　几秒钟过后，那个穿绿色西服的男人从谷仓

A to Z 神秘案件

前门冲了进来。丁丁在阁楼上能听见他的喘气声。

谷仓里光线很暗,那个男人朝周围看了看,然后从敞开的后门跑了出去。

丁丁松了口气,差点笑出声来。他刚想站起来,突然,露丝猛地把他往后一拉,让他趴下。

一个空信封

　　那个男人又跑回来了，他站在谷仓中央，像条蛇一样转着头四处张望。

　　丁丁和露丝一动不动，小心翼翼地从阁楼边缘往下看。

　　片刻之后，那个男人踢倒了一个桶，然后跺着脚离开了谷仓。

　　丁丁咽了一口唾沫，长长舒了一口气。他闭上眼睛，直到听到乔希在干草堆里小声说"他走了"，才睁开紧闭的双眼。

　　丁丁往下看，看到乔希从干草堆里

探出头,红色的头发上沾了很多干草——他看起来就像一个稻草人。

丁丁放下绳梯,和露丝顺着绳梯往下爬,感觉自己的腿都不听使唤了。

他们扑通一声落在乔希旁边的干草堆里。"我们现在该怎么办?"丁丁问,"那个怪人一定会回去,坐在我家门口的。"

孩子们坐在阴凉的谷仓里,努力想办法。突然,露丝坐直了身体。

"我想我知道该怎样证明多丽丝·邓肯和欧·伯德偷了那张邮票了。"她说,"如果事情顺利,法伦警官会立刻逮捕他们。"

"怎样证明?"丁丁和乔希一起问。

"我需要打个电话。"露丝说,"我们能去你家打电话吗,乔希?"

乔希从干草堆爬出来,往谷仓门外看了看,说:"外面没人。"

乔希悄悄打开门,他们穿过他家后院,跑进了厨房。

"你有什么计划?"丁丁问露丝。

一个空信封

露丝把她的计划告诉了他们。

乔希在空中挥了挥手臂。"这真是太棒了!"他大叫道。

丁丁睁大双眼,然后咧嘴笑道:"完美!如果你的计划成功实施,那张邮票就会重回它的主人手中,而那两个骗子就得去坐牢。"

露丝先给法伦警官打了电话。

她向法伦警官说了有关那几封信、那张被盗的邮票的情况和她的计划,丁丁和乔希一直在旁边听着。

露丝听着电话,然后开始点头:"嗯。明白。是的,好的,再见!"

"警官怎么说?"丁丁问。

露丝朝丁丁竖了一下大拇指,然后又给信息台打电话,问到了香格里拉酒店的电话号码。

她拨通了酒店的电话,问道:"请问多丽丝·邓肯是住在这儿吗?"

露丝朝丁丁和乔希咧嘴一笑,用口型无声地告诉他们:"他们刚进门。"

露丝开始和电话那边的人对话了,她的声音

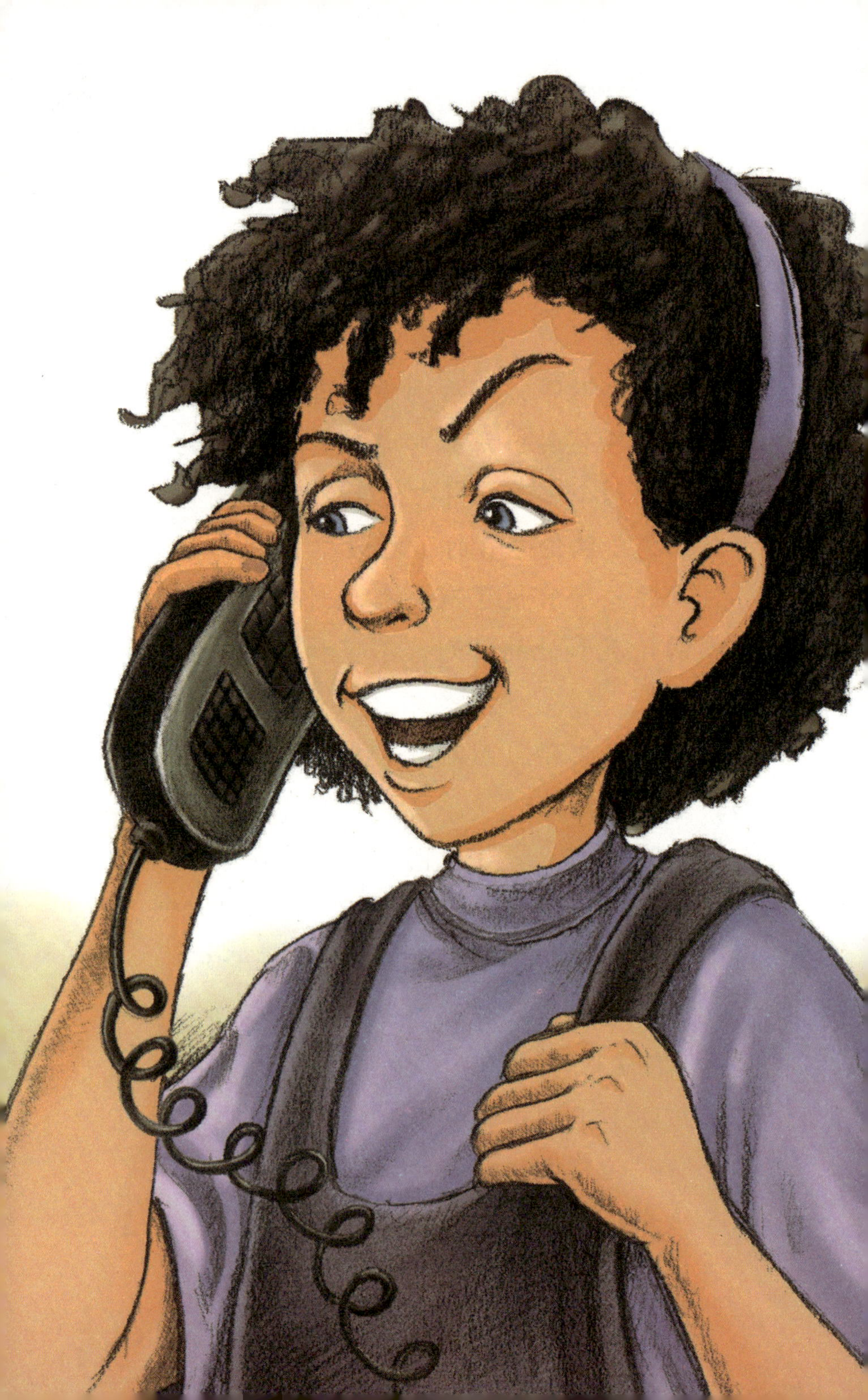

一个空信封

听起来像个坏男孩的腔调。

丁丁和乔希一起听着，惊讶得张大了嘴。

"你好，多丽丝·邓肯女士，我叫露丝。我是丁丁的朋友，你想要的那几封信在我手里。"

露丝冲男孩们做了个鬼脸，然后继续说："你的邮票也在我手里，就是那张飞机颠倒的邮票。"

接着，她压低声音说："我知道这张邮票值很多钱！"

露丝听对面说了一会儿，继续说道："丁丁很

A to Z 神秘案件

笨,他根本不知道那张邮票很值钱,我要把邮票五百美元卖给你。"

丁丁和乔希突然咧着嘴笑起来,丁丁不得不努力控制自己以免笑出声来。

露丝用另一只手做了一个嘘声的动作:"不,今天晚上不行,我要去我外祖母家,我们明天中午到图书馆见面吧。"

乔希憋着笑,差点倒在地上。

"不用担心。"露丝说,"我会带上那张邮票,而你只需要带五百美元过来。"

露丝说完就挂断了电话。

"露丝!"乔希大叫道,"你说话时就像个真正的骗子,你是怎么做到的?"

露丝微笑着说:"我真正的本事,你还没见过呢!"

第八章

第二天中午,丁丁和乔希在迈克尔罗伊太太的办公室里偷偷向外张望,露丝坐在一张桌子旁看书。

图书馆里没什么人。一位老妇人坐在里面看报纸,一个男人用帽子盖住眼睛在门口打盹。迈克尔罗伊太太出去吃午餐了。

"露丝看起来很镇定。"丁丁小声说,"我感觉我紧张得要吐了。"

"如果你真的吐出来,看我怎么收拾你。"乔希咧着嘴笑着说,"此外,迈克尔罗伊太太还会把你的借书卡取消。"

过了一会儿,多丽丝·邓肯走进图书馆,那个穿绿色西服的男人跟在她身后。他的手臂又长又壮,脖子很粗。

丁丁浑身打战,这个男人正是那个追过他们的男人。这两个人走进图书馆时,丁丁用手肘碰了乔希一下。

"你是露丝吗?"丁丁听到多丽丝·邓肯这样问道。

露丝点了点头,手里拿着那五个蓝色信封。"邮票在信封里面。"她一边说,一边让多丽丝·邓肯看那个空信封。

"我真希望露丝能先拿到钱。"乔希小声说。

露丝看了一眼那个男人,挑了挑眉毛,问:"他是谁?"她说话时用的是坏孩子的语气。

"这是我的同伴。"多丽丝·邓肯说,"欧托·伯德先生。"

"啊哈!"丁丁在办公室里说。

"你带钱了吗?"露丝问。

那个女人打了个响指,欧托·伯德马上从他

一个空信封

的口袋里抽出几张纸币递给多丽丝·邓肯。

"先让我看看那张邮票。"那个男人粗声粗气地说。

乔希忍不住咯咯笑出声来,丁丁立刻用手捂住他的嘴。

露丝把那张邮票从信封里倒了出来。

"看!邮票上有颠倒的飞机。"丁丁听到露丝这样说。

欧托·伯德一只手从露丝手上夺过邮票,另一只手则拿出一个放大镜。

那个男人瞪大眼睛检查那张邮票,然后他得意地笑着说:"就是那张邮票。"

露丝甜甜一笑。"给钱吧!"她说。

多丽丝·邓肯把五张一百美元的钞票扔在了露丝手里。

办公室里的丁丁和乔希击掌庆祝。

露丝大声数着钱,数完钱后,她看向多丽丝·邓肯和欧托·伯德。

随后她大叫起来:"好了,法伦警官!"

靠在门口打盹的那个男人站了起来。

A to Z 神秘案件

"你们俩别动!"法伦警官命令道,"你们因偷窃罪和邮政欺诈罪被捕了!"

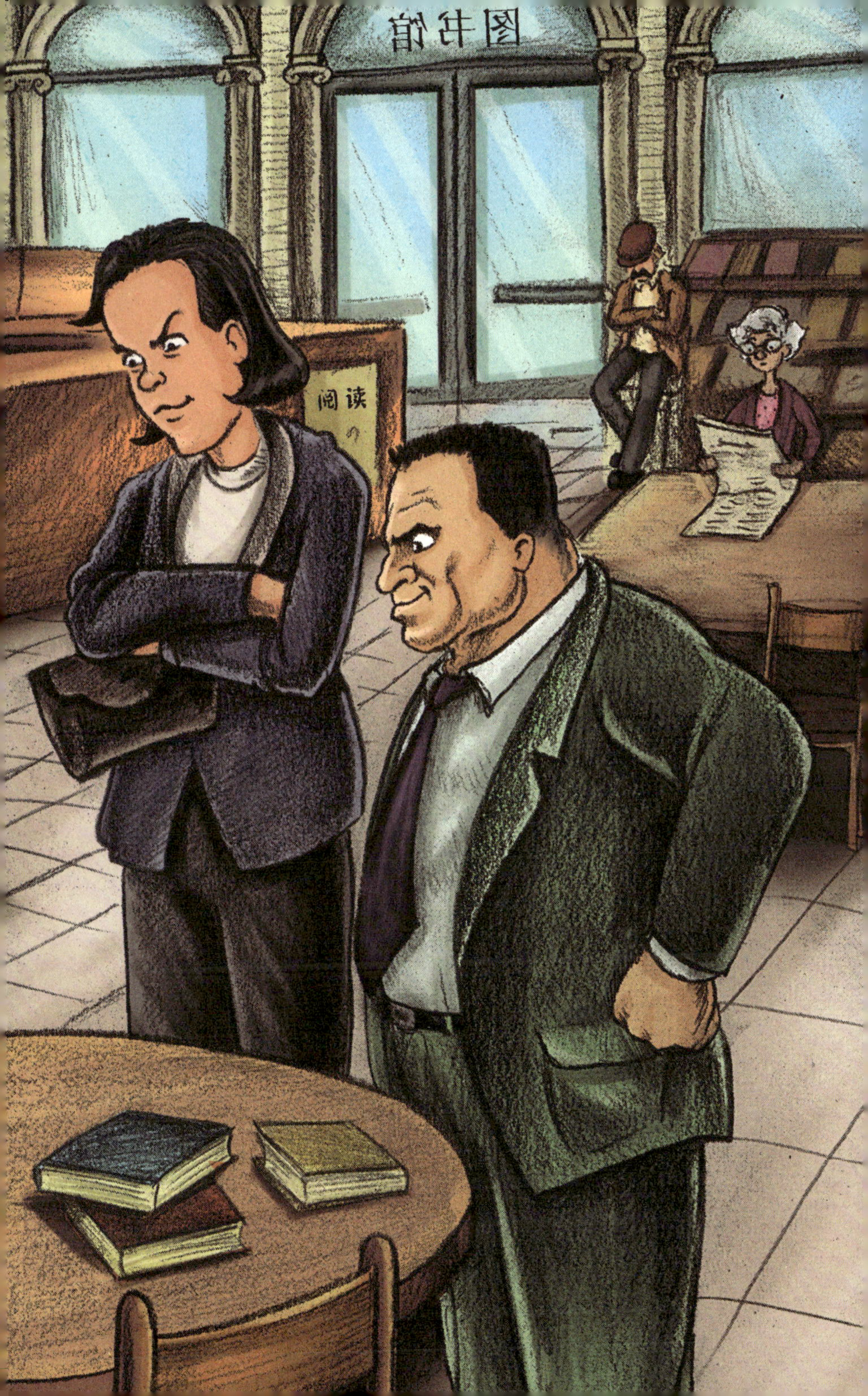

图书馆
阅读

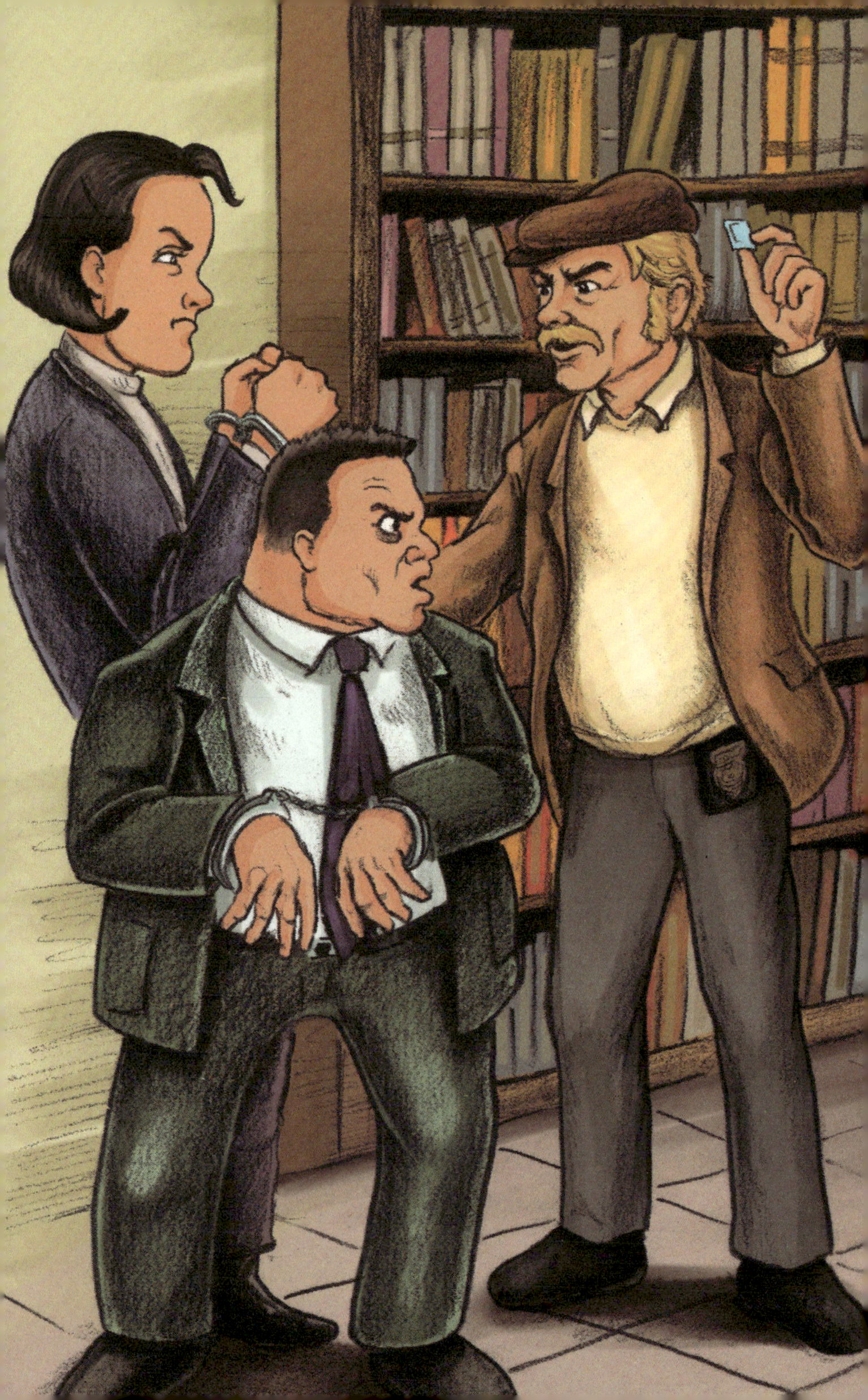

第九章

法伦警官给那两个窃贼戴上了手铐。

"邮票就由我来保管。"法伦警官一边说,一边把欧托手上的珍妮邮票接了过去。

多丽丝·邓肯恶狠狠地看了露丝一眼,她尖声大叫:"你竟然欺骗我们!"

一直在看报纸的老妇人突然站起身来。她一头银发,穿着一条漂亮的粉色碎花长裙。

老妇人把报纸折起来放在桌上,然后,她走

了过来。

"不,是你们骗了我!"老妇人说道。她转过身对欧托·伯德说:"还记得我——克莱芒蒂娜·潘特尔吗?你欺骗了我,你对我说你是邮票专家,但你就是个大骗子!"

欧托·伯德认出克莱芒蒂娜·潘特尔时,惊讶地张大了嘴,说不出话来。

办公室里,丁丁和乔希围着迈克尔罗伊太太的办公桌手舞足蹈。"抓到啦!"丁丁大叫道。

前一天,露丝和法伦警官通电话时,法伦警官说他会给克莱芒蒂娜·潘特尔打电话。法伦警官还解释道,有克莱芒蒂娜·潘特尔在场,多丽丝·邓肯和欧托·伯德就不会得逞。

为了取回她的邮票,克莱芒蒂娜踏上了前往绿地镇的公交车。

丁丁和乔希从办公室里走出来时,多丽丝·邓肯睁大了微微斜视的眼睛,然后她紧闭双眼,就像头痛发作了一样。

欧托·伯德的脸色变得像他的领带一样紫。丁丁想,这个男人要气炸了。

一个空信封

"你们没有证据！"欧托·伯德大叫，举起戴着手铐的手，指着多丽丝说，"是她策划了这一切——。"

"闭嘴，青蛙脸！"多丽丝·邓肯厉声对欧托·伯德喊道，"要是你抄对了邮政编码，我们也不会栽在这个'一文不名'的绿地镇上。"

法伦警官轻声笑了："不用担心，你们不会在这个'一文不名'的绿地镇待很久，我听说纽约可是有价值百万的监狱。"

法伦警官押着两个邮票窃贼往门口走去。"一个小时后，在埃莉餐馆见！"他转过头对孩子们说。

孩子们和克莱芒蒂娜走到窗户边，他们看见法伦警官押着两个窃贼穿过街道进入警察局。

"天哪！"克莱芒蒂娜对孩子们说，"这太刺激了，比电视上演的还刺激！"

一个小时后，大家在埃莉餐馆会面了，克莱芒蒂娜请孩子们吃冰激凌。

"能请别人吃东西的感觉真好！"克莱芒蒂娜

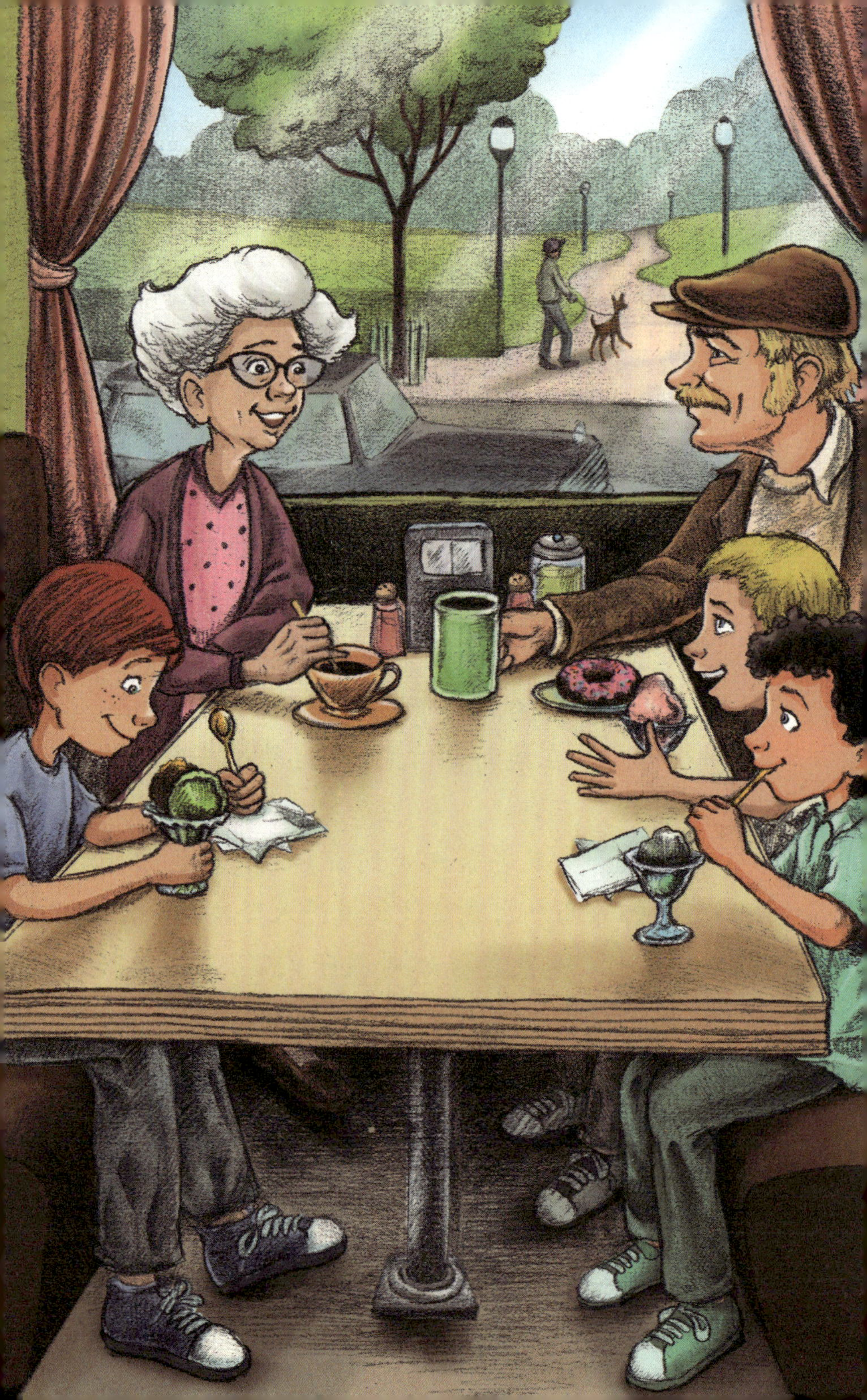

一个空信封

说,"我以为我永远找不回我的邮票了。"

"那张邮票是怎么跑到您的吸尘器里去的?"丁丁问。

克莱芒蒂娜微微笑了笑,不过她的笑容里流露出悲伤:"我妈妈最近去世了,她已经九十六岁了。我在清理她的旧真空吸尘器时发现了那张邮票。她肯定是使用吸尘器时不小心把那张邮票吸进去的。不过,谁知道她是什么时候、在哪儿把那张邮票吸进去的呢?"

"您怎么知道那张邮票很值钱?"露丝问。

"我一开始也不知道!"克莱芒蒂娜说,"但我知道那张邮票年头很久了,所以我在电话簿上查到了一个邮票协会的电话。"她摇了摇头,"自那以后,麻烦就开始了。"

法伦警官点了点头。"欧托说得很好听。"法伦警官说,"他好像就在您打电话的协会工作,您打电话咨询邮票的信息时,就是他接的电话。"

"他真的非常有礼貌!"克莱芒蒂娜说,"他还让我把那张邮票藏起来,他会马上来看邮票。"

克莱芒蒂娜生气地说:"他说他要看那张邮票,

77

而我就像个老笨蛋，给他看了我藏邮票的地方。"

"您把邮票藏在哪儿了？"乔希问。

克莱芒蒂娜脸红了。"藏在饼干盒里了。"她说，"我每天都要就着茶吃一块饼干。"

丁丁哈哈大笑："那张邮票可真是什么地方都待过了！"

"我不明白那张邮票怎么会跑到其他邮票下面。"克莱芒蒂娜说。

"欧托·伯德把它藏在普通邮票下面了，这样他就可以把它邮寄到科罗拉多州的多丽丝·邓肯家。"法伦警官解释道，"他们计划把那张邮票卖掉，然后平分五万美元。"

"可是，欧托·伯德为什么要写那些信呢？"丁丁问。

"他们俩以前都有案底。"法伦警官说，"为了预防有人打开信件，他们得让自己看起来是清白无辜的，这就是为什么欧托·伯德在那些信中署名'妈妈'。"

"多丽丝·邓肯收到信后，她就知道到哪里去找到那张邮票。"露丝说。

一个空信封

"可是她没有收到信啊!"乔希说。

法伦警官微笑着说:"没错,潘特尔小姐非常幸运,欧托的眼镜摔坏了,他把科罗拉多州绿地镇的邮政编码抄成了康涅狄格州绿地镇的邮政编码。"

"后来,我的弟弟还把信藏到了冰箱里!"露丝补充道。

"天哪!"克莱芒蒂娜说,"因为一张小小的纸片,竟然发生了这么多事情。"

法伦警官拿出一个信封,递到桌子另一边。"这是您的邮票,潘特尔小姐。"他笑着说,"您能找个更安全的地方把它藏起来吗?"

"当然,警官!"她说,"我马上把它存放到银行去。"

大家互相道了别,法伦警官把克莱芒蒂娜送到公交车站。

孩子们也朝家里走去,边走边谈论着在真空吸尘器里找到一大笔财富的事情。

"还想到我家打排球吗?"丁丁问。

"当然。昨天我和纳特赢了呢!"露丝说。

A to Z 神秘案件

乔希咧着嘴笑了:"我就不去了。我要马上回家,去看看我妈妈的真空吸尘器里有什么!"

A to Z Mysteries®

The Empty Envelope

by Ron Roy

illustrated by
John Steven Gurney

INDIAN RIVER
LAWRENCE TAXI
RIVER ROAD
HORSE TRAILS
HORSES FOR RENT
BIKE PATH
WOODS
WOODVIEW ROAD
INDIAN WAY ROAD
FIRE STATION
BILL'S BIKES
SUPER MARKET
BIKE PATH
BRIDGE LANE
ROBIN ROAD
CROW ST
FINCH LA
THRUSH CT
OWL RD
PHEASANT LA
BLUE JAY WAY
WREN DR
FITNESS CENTER
WOODS
BIKE PATH
BLUE BIRD WAY
HUMMINGBIRD LA
WOODCOCK CROSS
ELLIE'S DINER
ACORN APTS
FURRY FEET PET SHOP
OAK STREET
CENTER CHURCH
BIKE PATH
PEOPLE'S POND
POST OFFICE
COMMUNITY GARDEN AND FISH POND
GREEN LAWN $ SAVINGS $ BANK
ELDERLY HOUSING
POLICE STATION
GOOSE ISLAND
RIVER ROAD
WEST GREEN St
GREEN LAWN LIBRARY
SENIOR COMMUNITY CENTER
TOWN HALL
MAIN STREET
BIKE PATH
CHILDREN'S PETTING ZOO AND AQUARIUM
SHANGRI-LA HOTEL

WELCOME TO
GREEN LAWN
HOME OF THE
A to Z Mysteries
N
W
E
S
RIVER ROAD
BOAT LAUNCH
BOAT RENTAL
RON'S BAIT
DUCK WALK WAY
GREEN LAWN MIDDLE SCHOOL
EAGLE LANE
FARM LANE
JOSH
SQUAW ISLAND
GREEN LAWN ELEMENTARY SCHOOL
DINK
RUTH ROSE
TREE TOP CIRCLE
MEADOW ROAD
FOX LANE
QUAIL RUN ROAD
SILVER CIRCLE
WOODY STREET
PLEASANT STREET
BAND SHELL
ROSE GARDEN
THISTLE COURT
WILDFLOWER WAY
CENTER PARK
ROSE STREET
GREEN LAWN HIGH SCHOOL
SWAN POND
PLAYING FIELDS
GYM + POOL
BOXWOOD LANE
HOWARD'S BARBER-SHOP
BOOK NOOK
CRYSTAL POND
GAS STATION
MYSTIC GREENHOUSE
DOG KENNEL + VETERINARIAN
RIVER ROAD
EAST GREEN STREET
TOWN TENNIS COURTS
TOWN SWIMMING POOL
KIDDIE POOL
TOWN BASEBALL FIELD
TO THE BLUE HILLS

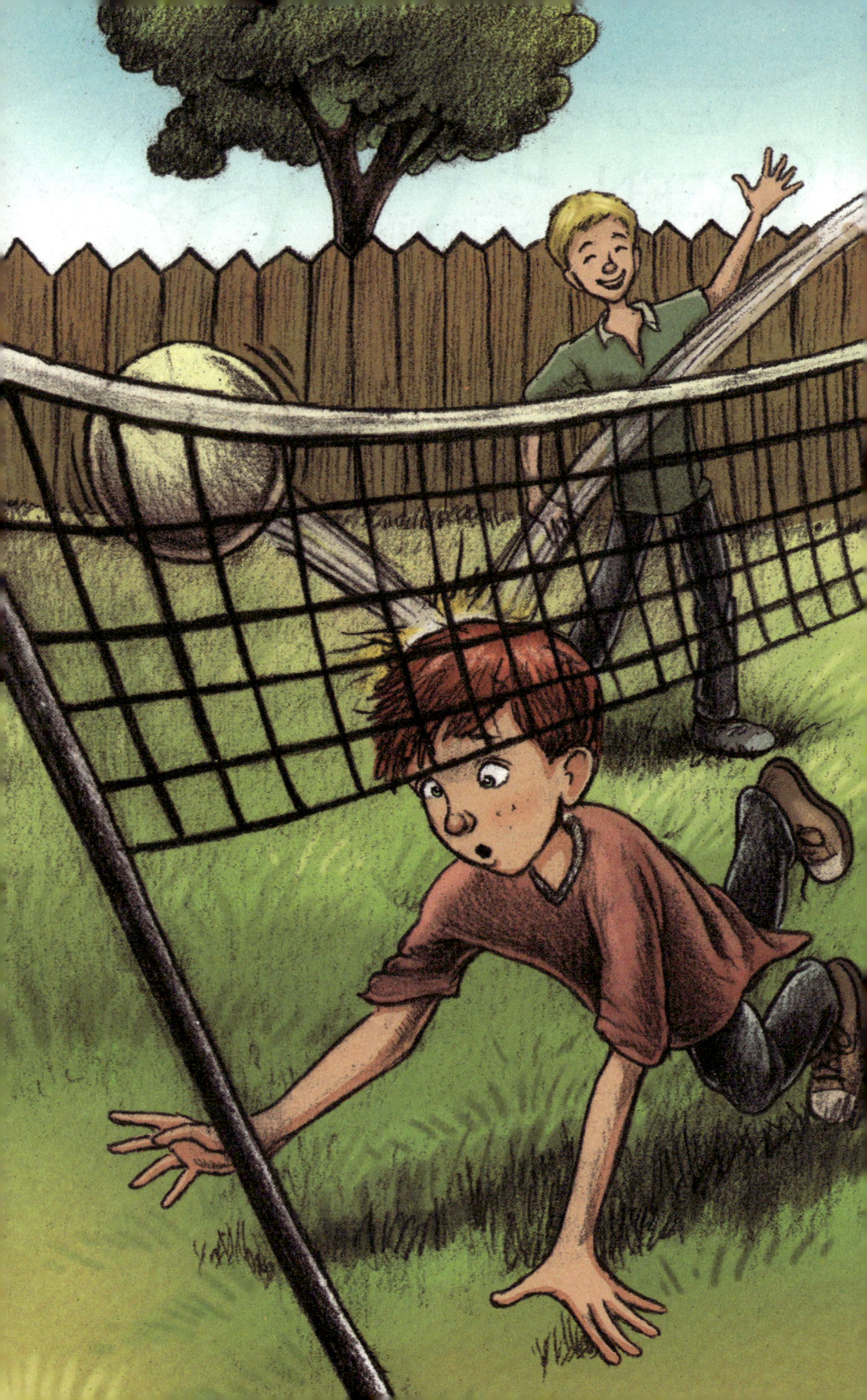

Chapter 1

"I got it! I got it!" Josh yelled as he raced across Dink's backyard. He leaped into the air, missed the volleyball, and fell in a heap.

Dink laughed. "You got it, all right!"

"Way to go, Natie!" Ruth Rose cried. She gave her four-year-old brother, Nate, a high five. "You just scored us another point!"

Nate blushed and smiled shyly at his big sister.

Josh got up and grinned. "Okay, I'm through foolin' around! From now on, Josh and Dink will rule!"

Just then they heard a beep. "It's Ruby with the mail," Ruth Rose said.

Josh dropped the volleyball. "I wonder if you'll get another blue envelope," he said to Dink. "I can't wait to read what Mother has to say today!"

Dink ran to the front just as Ruby waved from her truck and drove away. He opened the mailbox and reached in.

He pulled out two bills for his parents and a letter in a blue envelope for him.

In the past week, Dink had received four other letters in blue envelopes. This was the fifth. Each envelope was addressed to D. Duncan, Green Lawn, CO 06040. But the notes inside were to someone named Doris—from her mother!

Dink returned to his backyard. He held the letter up. "Another one," he said.

"Well, open it," Josh said.

Dink ripped open the envelope and felt inside for

一个空信封

the note.

"There's nothing in here," he said. "It's empty."

Ruth Rose peered into the envelope. "Why would Mother send an empty envelope?" she asked.

Dink shrugged. "Let's go in the house. I want to check out the other letters again."

The kids trooped into Dink's kitchen. A covered plate sat on the counter.

"My mom made us some sandwiches," Dink said.

Nate reached for the plate, but his sister stopped him. "Look at those hands! Let's wash up at the sink, Nate."

Dink pulled the other four envelopes from a drawer and laid them on the table side by side. They all looked the same.

"Can I get some juice?" Josh opened the fridge before Dink could answer.

Dink just nodded as he sat and stared at the envelopes. The return address on each was O. Bird, 10 Carroll St. , Brooklyn, NY 11234. "I don't know anyone in Brooklyn," he said, "let alone someone named O. Bird."

A to Z 神秘案件

```
O. Bird
10 Carroll St.
Brooklyn, NY 11234

              D. Duncan
              Green Lawn, CO
              06040
```

Dink dropped his eyes to the middle of one of the envelopes. "Hey, look at this!" he said suddenly. He pointed to the CO in his address. "Isn't CO the abbreviation for Colorado?"

Josh and Ruth Rose each grabbed an envelope.

"Yeah, you're right," Josh said. "Connecticut is CT, not CO."

Dink looked at his friends. "The zip code is right, but the state is wrong!"

"Or maybe it's the state that's right and the zip code that's wrong," Ruth Rose suggested.

一个空信封

"What do you mean?" Josh asked.

"Maybe these letters were supposed to go to some D. Duncan in Green Lawn, Colorado," Ruth Rose said. "Whoever O. Bird is just wrote down the wrong zip code."

"I know how to find out," Dink said.

He walked over to the phone and dialed information. He asked the long-distance operator for O. Bird's number.

"There isn't?" he said. "Okay, thanks anyway." Dink hung up. "There's no O. Bird listed in Brooklyn."

"Well," Josh said, grabbing a sandwich, "you're the only D. Duncan in Green Lawn."

"In Green Lawn, Connecticut," Dink said.

Josh sighed. "Anyway, let's eat."

They wolfed down the peanut butter and grape jam sandwiches.

"Read the notes again, Dink," Ruth Rose said after a few minutes. "Maybe there's a clue about who they're really meant for."

Dink opened the envelopes, pulled out the four notes, and laid them side by side.

89

A to Z 神秘案件

Josh picked up the fifth envelope. He turned it upside down and shook it. "Maybe someone stole the last letter," he whispered. He made mysterious eyes at Dink.

"Maybe spies are watching your mail," he said in a creepy voice. "Maybe they're alien kidnappers from

JULY 1

DEAR DORIS,
I SAW JENNY LAST WEEK. SHE LOOKS SO PRETTY AND SENDS HER LOVE. I BROKE MY GLASSES, BUT I'M HAVING THEM FIXED.
SEE YOU SOON,
MOTHER

JULY 3

DEAR DORIS
THE KIDS CAME FOR SUNDAY LUNCH. THEY WERE SO CUTE. SALLY HID IN THE DEN AND MADE THE REST OF US SEARCH FOR HER.
MORE LATER,
LOVE, MOTHER

一个空信封

Neptune and. . ."

Just then the phone rang.

DEAR DORIS, JULY 5
I THOUGHT OF YOU ON YOUR BIRTHDAY. A SURPRISE IS COMING SOON. KEEP SMILING!
LOVE,
MOTHER

DEAR DORIS, JULY 7
LITTLE KATE HAD HER FIFTH BIRTHDAY LAST WEEK. I PUT SOME MONEY IN AN ENVELOPE FROM BOTH OF US. SHE WAS THRILLED!
HOPE ALL IS WELL. LOVE,
MOTHER

Chapter 2

Dink answered the phone.

"Is this D. Duncan?" a woman's voice asked.

"I'm Donald Duncan," Dink said. "But my friends call me Dink."

"Well, Dink," the voice said, "I'm Doris Duncan from Colorado. I think you may have some letters that belong to me."

Dink covered the phone and turned to Josh and Ruth Rose. "It's some woman from Colorado asking for the letters!" he whispered excitedly.

"Hello? Are you still there?" the woman asked.

一个空信封

"Don't hang up!"

Dink spoke into the phone again. "Um…I got five blue envelopes this week."

"Well, those letters are mine. They're very important," Doris Duncan said. "When can I get them back?"

Dink glanced across the kitchen. "They're right here on the table," he told Doris Duncan. "Do you want me to send them to you?"

"No!" the woman snapped. "Don't send them anywhere! I'm at the Shangri-la Hotel right now. How do I find you?"

"Well, I guess you could come to my house," Dink said. He gave her directions to 22 Woody Street and hung up.

"What was that all about?" Ruth Rose asked.

Dink sat at the table again. "That was Doris Duncan. The letters are hers, and she's coming right over to get them."

"From Colorado?" Josh said.

"No, she's at the Shangri-la. She should be here in a few minutes."

"She's in Connecticut?" Ruth Rose said. "That's weird."

Dink nodded. "Yeah, and another thing. She sounded mad, like I took the letters on purpose."

"This is so lame," Josh said, yawning. "You got the letters by mistake, and some woman is coming over to get them." He stood up and stretched. "Let's go finish the game."

Dink slipped the notes back inside their envelopes, then stood them between the salt and pepper shakers.

Ruth Rose poked the envelopes. "Don't you guys think it's weird that she came all the way to Connecticut just for some notes from her mom?"

"Maybe Dink can ask her when she gets here," Josh said. "Now can we please play volleyball?"

Ruth Rose stood up. "What could be so important about these letters?" she wondered out loud.

Ten minutes later, Dink heard someone calling, "You there, young man!"

Dink ran to the side yard and saw a tall woman walking up his sidewalk. He jogged out front to meet

一个空信封

her.

"Hi. Are you Mrs. Duncan?"

The woman towered over Dink. "I'm Ms. Duncan. Are you Dink?"

Dink had to bend his head backward to see the tall woman's face. She had black hair and dark, squinty eyes. She was clutching a purse in her large, strong-looking hand.

"Well, are you the boy I talked to or not?" the woman demanded.

Dink gulped. "Yes, ma'am. I'll get the letters," he said.

"Thank you," the woman said. Suddenly she sounded almost nice. "They're from my mother, Bessie Duncan. She died last month. These were her last letters to me."

Dink went inside to the kitchen. He walked over to the table to get the letters. But they were gone!

Dink looked around the kitchen. The letters weren't on the counter, the fridge, or the stove.

Dink looked on the floor under the table. He saw a few crumbs from lunch, but no blue envelopes.

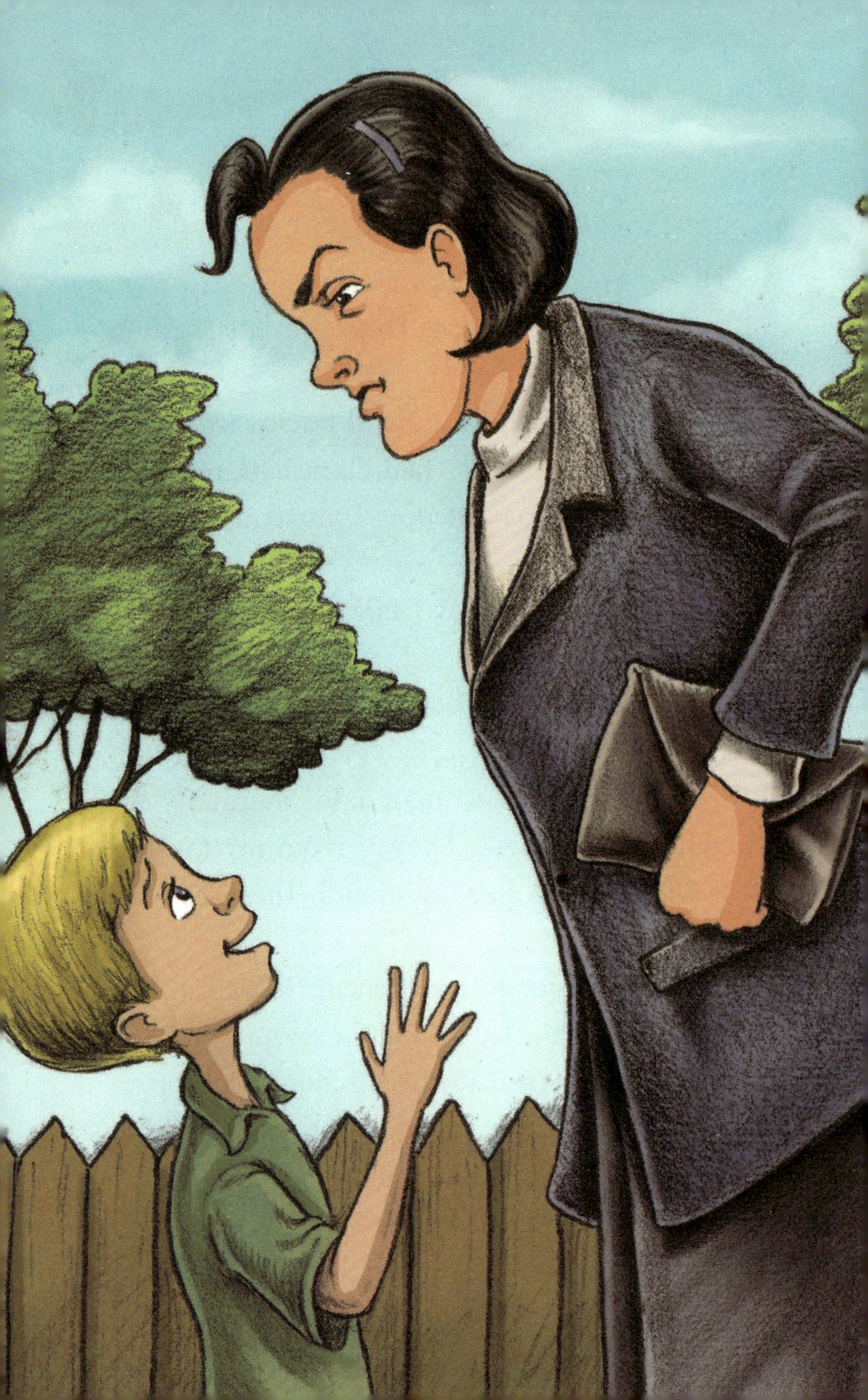

一个空信封

"What's the matter?" Ruth Rose said. She and Josh were peering through the back screen door.

"I can't find the letters!" Dink told his friends. "Didn't I leave them on the table after we ate lunch?"

Ruth Rose pushed open the door and came in. "I think so."

She looked behind the toaster, the coffee maker, and the microwave.

"Help us look, Josh," Dink said. "That lady is waiting! The letters are from her mom, and she died last month!"

Josh stepped inside, and the kids searched the kitchen. The letters had vanished.

"Guess I'd better go tell her," Dink muttered, shaking his head. "I know I left them on the table!"

He walked through the living room and opened the front door. Doris Duncan was standing where he'd left her.

Dink swallowed. "I…um, I'm real sorry, but I can't find the letters."

The woman glared down at him. "What do you mean?" she said. "When I called, you said you had them. Where are they?"

Dink felt his face turn red. "I don't know," he mumbled. "They were on the kitchen table, and now they're not. My friends even helped me look."

The woman stared over Dink's shoulder. She looked as if she wanted to barge past him and search the house herself.

"I'll ask my mom to help when she gets home," Dink said. "Can you come back later?"

Doris Duncan tapped her fingers on her purse. "I'll be back at six o'clock sharp," she said. "I'll expect my letters then, young man!"

"Don't worry, we'll find them," Dink assured her. "My mom can find anything. She's a real neat Nelly!"

The woman sniffed, then stomped down the sidewalk toward the street.

Dink watched her go, then turned around and bumped into Josh.

"I'm telling your mom you called her a neat Nelly," Josh said, grinning.

"It's not polite to listen to people's conversations, Joshua," Dink said. He headed back to the kitchen.

一个空信封

"Guys, look at this," Ruth Rose said. She was pointing at a small purple handprint on the kitchen table. "I thought I wiped the table."

Josh bent over and sniffed the purple print. "It's grape jam."

Ruth Rose grinned. "I think I know who took the envelopes," she said.

Chapter 3

The kids marched next door to Ruth Rose's house. They found Nate in the living room watching a video. His fingers and mouth were stained purple.

"Natie, did you take Dink's letters?" Ruth Rose asked.

Nate looked at his sister with big blue eyes. He shook his head. "Nope."

Ruth Rose glanced at Dink and Josh. She rolled her eyes. "Okay, then who took them? We found your jammy fingerprints."

Nate hid his hands under his T-shirt. "Steggy did,"

一个空信封

he said softly.

Dink knelt down next to Nate. "Where did Steggy put the envelopes?" he asked.

Nate shrugged, watching two dancing dinosaurs on TV.

"Who the heck is Steggy?" Josh asked.

"His favorite dinosaur," Ruth Rose said. She turned off the TV. "Natie, Dink really needs his letters. Can you show us where Steggy put them?"

Nate let out a big sigh. He got up and walked into the kitchen. The kids followed.

Nate pulled open the refrigerator door. A stuffed stegosaur sat on a shelf next to a bowl of strawberry Jell-O.

Steggy had five blue envelopes in his mouth.

Josh laughed. "Yo, Nate, don't you know dinosaurs hate the cold?"

Nate pulled Steggy off the shelf and shut the door. "Steggy's playing mailman. It's hot outside," he said.

Ruth Rose handed the envelopes to Dink. "It's not nice to take things without asking," she told her brother.

A to Z 神秘案件

"It's okay, Natie," Dink said, examining the envelopes for purple smudges. He wanted the letters to look perfect for Doris Duncan.

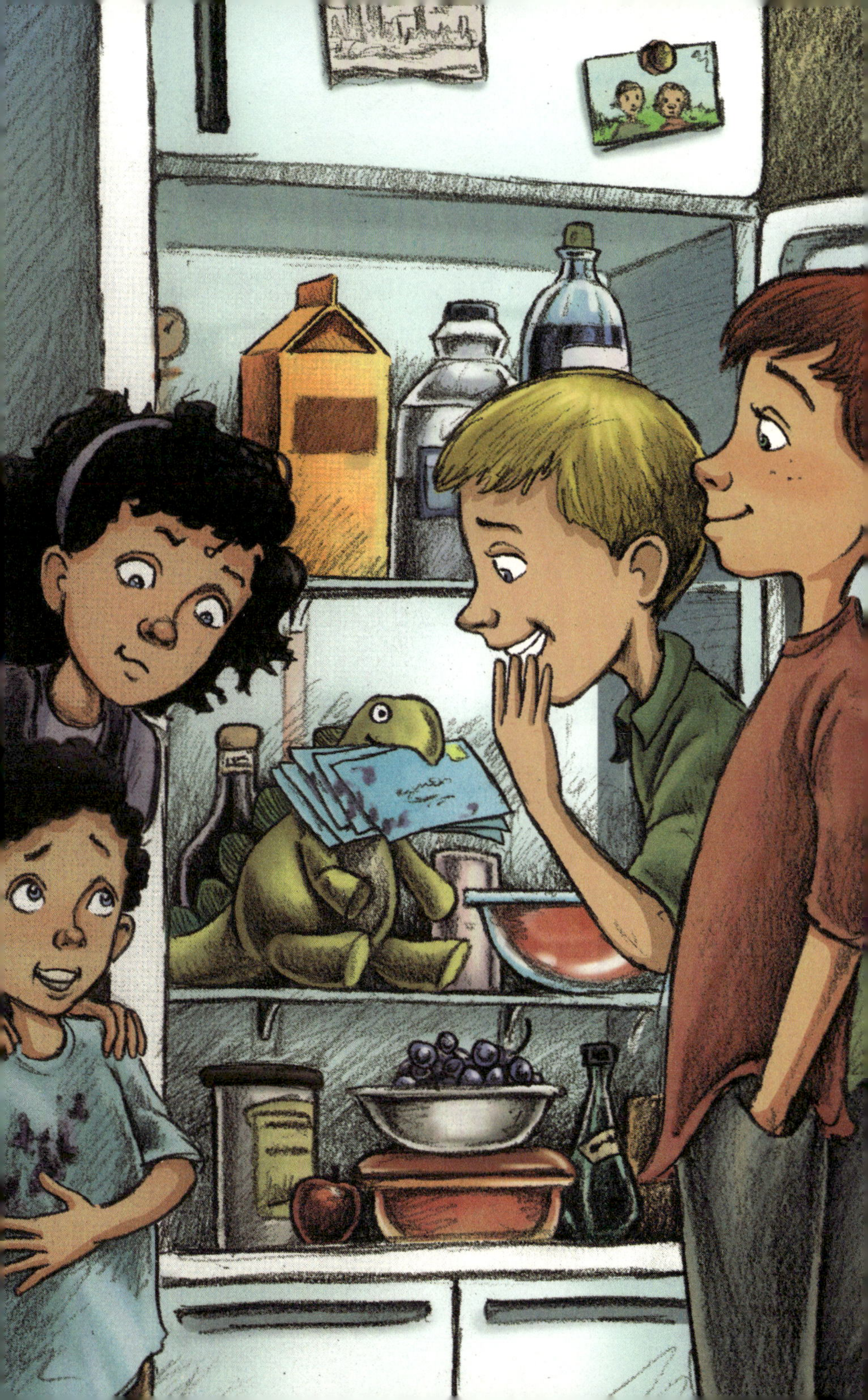

Dink found a few splotches of grape jam and wiped them off on his pants. When he looked for more purple stains, he noticed the return address again.

"This is weird," he said.

Dink showed the return address to Josh and Ruth Rose. "Doris Duncan's mother's name is Bessie Duncan. So why are the letters from O. Bird?"

"Maybe O. Bird mailed the notes for her after she died," Josh said.

Dink laid the envelopes in a row on the kitchen table. He pulled out the notes and placed them next to their envelopes.

"But what about this?" Dink said. "The letters are all dated last week. But Doris Duncan told me her mom died last month!"

"Mind if I get us all some milk?" Josh asked.

"Go ahead," Ruth Rose said, picking up the empty envelope. "And why would anyone send her own daughter an envelope with nothing in it?"

Dink nodded. "It doesn't make any sense," he said, "unless these letters aren't really from her mother."

104

一个空信封

"But why would Doris tell us a story like that?" Ruth Rose wondered.

Josh picked up one of the letters. He read it quickly. Then he carefully spilled a small puddle of milk on the writing.

"What're you doing!" Dink yelled. "Doris Duncan will kill me!"

"Wait a sec." Josh smeared the milk around with his finger. "I read in a spy comic that if you pour milk on invisible ink, you can read it," he said. "Maybe there's a secret message!"

They all hunched over the letter. No hidden writing appeared. But now there was a wet, milky blotch over some of the words.

"Thanks a lot, Josh," Dink said. "Wait till Doris Duncan sees this!"

Ruth Rose blotted the letter with a paper napkin. "Don't worry, it'll dry," she said. She waved the letter in the air, then held it up to the sunny window.

"It'd better," Dink said, giving Josh an "or you'll be sorry!" look.

"Guys, look at this!" Ruth Rose said. "There are

two pinholes in the paper. The holes go right through the letters H and D!"

Josh grabbed another letter. He held it next to Ruth Rose's at the window. "This one has a hole too!" he said.

"There's a tiny one right through the letter J!"

Dink jumped up and looked at the pinholes. Then he stared at his friends. "Maybe there really is a secret message!" he said.

Chapter 4

The kids examined the other two notes. They found pinholes through the letters O, F, and E.

"H, D, J, O, F, and E all have holes through them," Dink said, writing the letters on a pad.

"Maybe the letters spell a secret message," Ruth Rose said. "Let's try to make words out of them." She grabbed the pad.

"I get hoe, Joe, doe, foe, and fed," she said after a minute.

"How about of, Ed, oh, and he," Dink suggested.

"Those words don't make any sense," Josh said.

"Maybe each letter stands for a word. You know, like SCUBA."

Dink and Ruth Rose just stared at him.

"You know, SCUBA? S, C, U, B, and A? The letters stand for 'self-contained underwater breathing apparatus.'"

Dink grinned. "Josh, how come you look so dumb, but you're really so smart?"

Josh grinned right back. "How come you look so dumb, and you really are?"

"Guys, stop fooling around," Ruth Rose said. "Let's figure out what these letters mean."

The kids spent ten minutes trying to make a message out of the letters J, H, D, O, F, and E.

"I give up," Dink said finally.

"Wait a minute," Josh said. "Maybe Mother's already shown us the secret words." He picked up one of the notes and peered at the pinholes. "Look," he said. "This hole is in the first E in envelope. Maybe it's the word envelope. that's part of the code!"

Dink and Ruth Rose arranged the four notes by date. Then they looked at the words next to the

108

一个空信封

pinholes.

Dink wrote down six words: Jenny, hid, den, on, fifth, envelope.

Ruth Rose started to read them out loud, then suddenly grinned. "Listen, guys. 'Jenny hidden on fifth envelope.'"

"Awesome!" Josh said, giving Ruth Rose a big grin.

"The one that came today is the fifth envelope," Dink said, holding it up. "But who—or what—is Jenny?"

"The message says Jenny is on the envelope," Josh said. "But all I see are the stamps."

"Don't forget the ink and glue," Dink said.

"What about looking for the letters J, E, N, N, and Y in the addresses?" Ruth Rose suggested.

"E, N, N, and Y are there," Josh said after a minute. "But there's no J."

"That leaves the stamps," Dink said. The stamps were pictures of big yellow sunflowers. "I don't see any Jenny there."

"Guys, look," Ruth Rose said. She grabbed the other envelopes. "The first four envelopes have just one stamp each. But the one that came today has three."

"You're right," Dink said. "I wonder why." He rubbed his fingers across the three sunflower stamps. "I feel something under there!" he said.

Dink held the envelope up to the window. "There's something dark under those stamps," he said. "I can see an outline!"

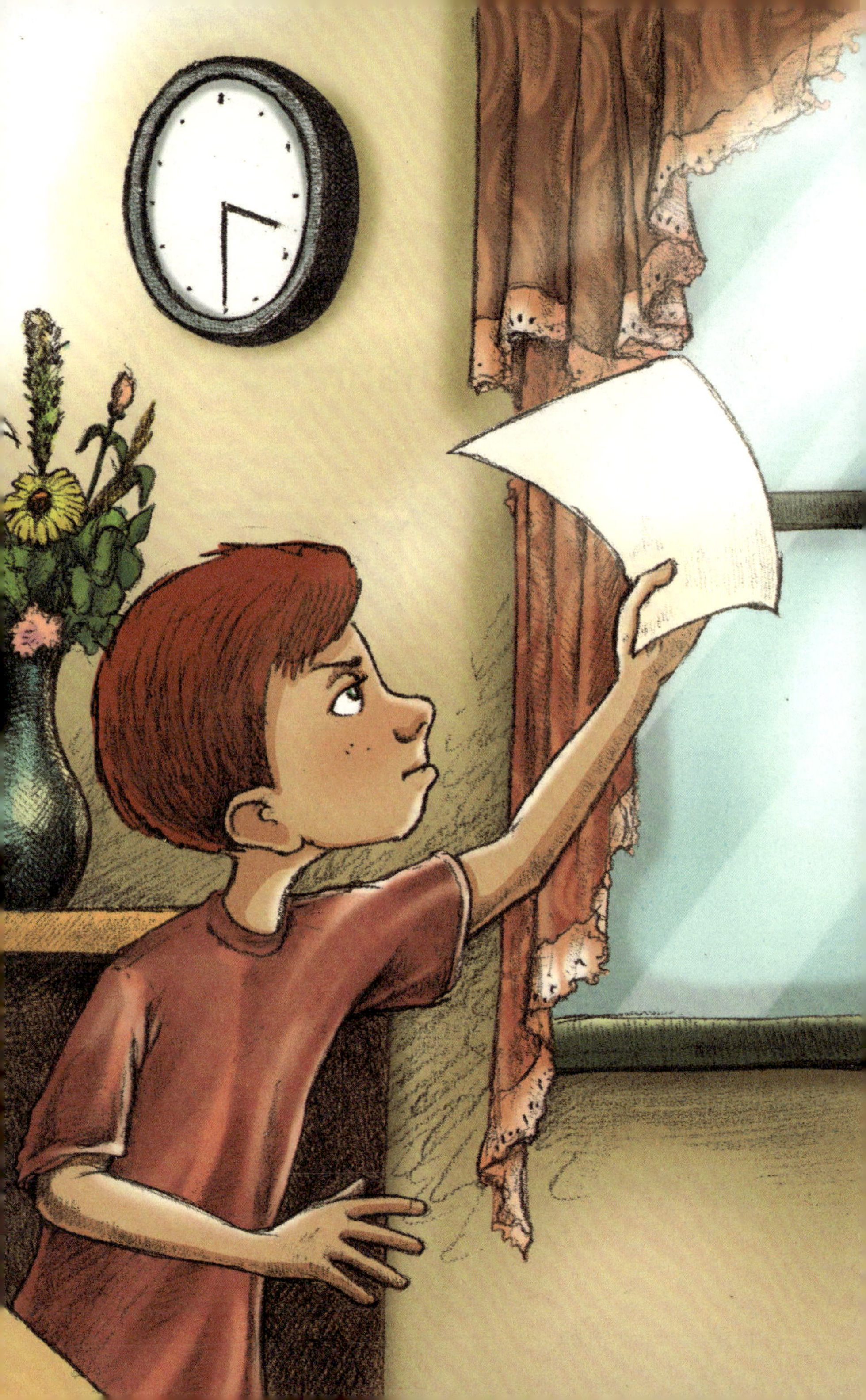

Chapter 5

"I'm going to boil some water," Ruth Rose said. "My grandfather used to collect stamps. He showed me how to steam 'em off envelopes."

Ruth Rose ran water into the teakettle and set the kettle on the burner. Then she turned on the stove.

The kids sat and stared at it.

"Sure is taking a long time to boil," Dink muttered, brushing his fingertips over the sunflower stamps.

Suddenly steam began whistling out of the kettle spout. Dink handed Ruth Rose the empty envelope.

Ruth Rose held the envelope so the stamps were

right over the kettle's spout.

In a few seconds, moisture began gathering on the stamps. Then the stamps began to peel away from the envelope.

"Cool!" Josh said. "I feel like a spy!"

Ruth Rose shut off the stove. Using the tip of a toothpick, she removed the three sunflower stamps from the envelope.

Hidden beneath the stamps, covered with cellophane, was a smaller stamp. It was blue. In the center of the stamp was a picture of an old-fashioned airplane. The plane was flying upside down.

Dink removed the cellophane. "It's an old stamp," he said.

Josh poked a finger at the stamp. "The dumb thing is printed wrong," he muttered. "What's the big deal about an upside-down airplane stamp?"

Ruth Rose studied the stamp. "Maybe it's valuable," she said. "My grandfather has a stamp that's worth two hundred dollars!"

"I wonder if Doris Duncan knew this was here," Dink said.

The kids looked at each other. Then they stared at the little blue stamp.

"We should go to the library and look at a book about stamps," Ruth Rose said finally.

Dink glanced at the kitchen clock. "We better

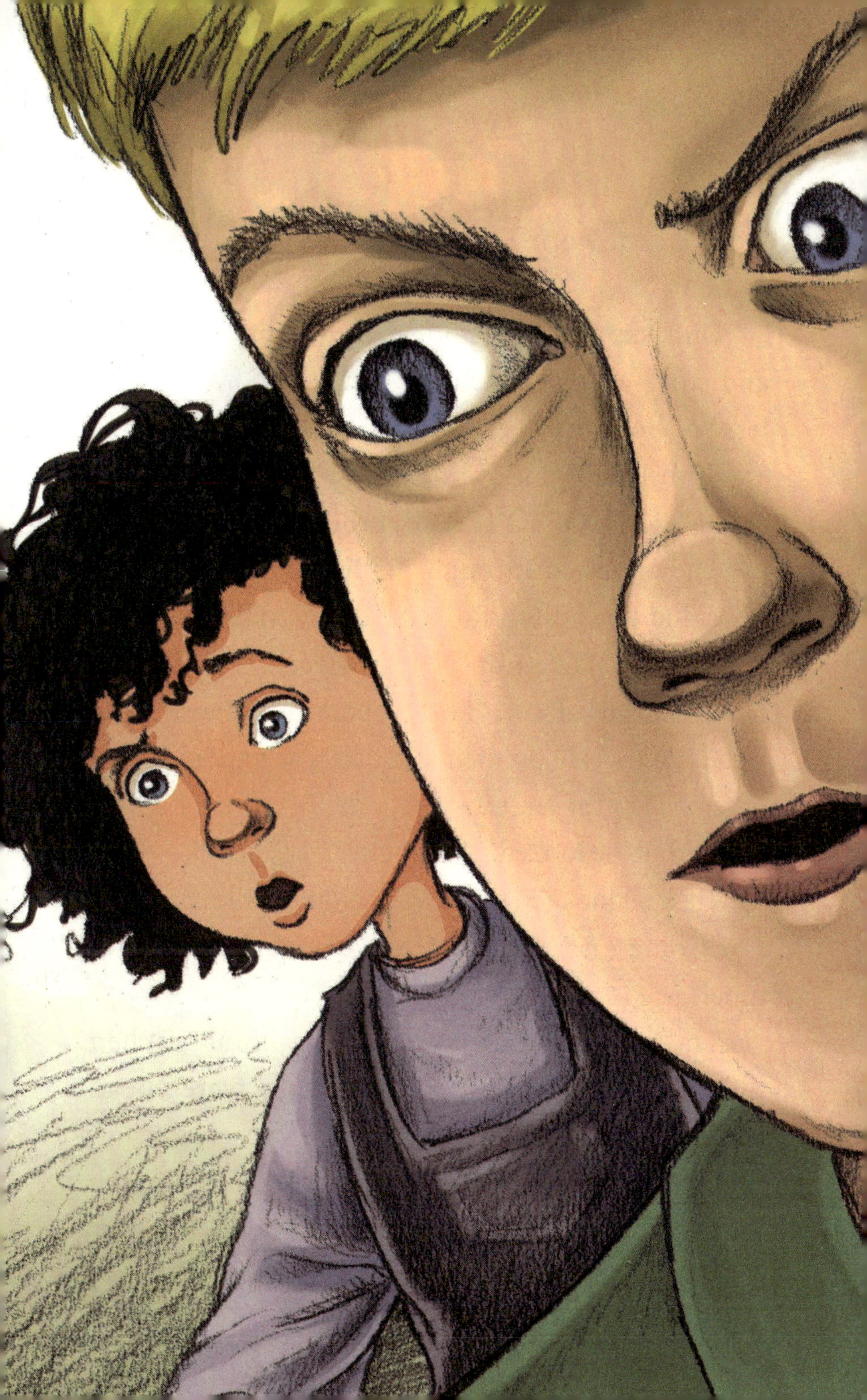

make it fast. Doris Duncan will be back in less than an hour!"

Dink slipped the stamp inside the empty envelope and stuck all five envelopes under his shirt. "Okay, let's go," he said.

Ruth Rose went to the bottom of the hall stairs. "MOM, I'M GOING TO THE LIBRARY!" she yelled.

They hurried through the living room, out the door, and down Ruth Rose's front sidewalk.

As they started up Woody Street, Josh nudged Dink with his elbow. "Look. There's some weird guy watching us." He pointed at a dark car parked on the other side of the street.

Ruth Rose looked. "What guy?"

They all looked. There was no one in the car.

"Come on," Dink said. "We're running out of time!"

The kids ran all the way to the library. When they charged up the front steps, they were out of breath.

Mrs. Mackleroy looked up as they burst through the door. "Slow down, kids," she said. "Why, your

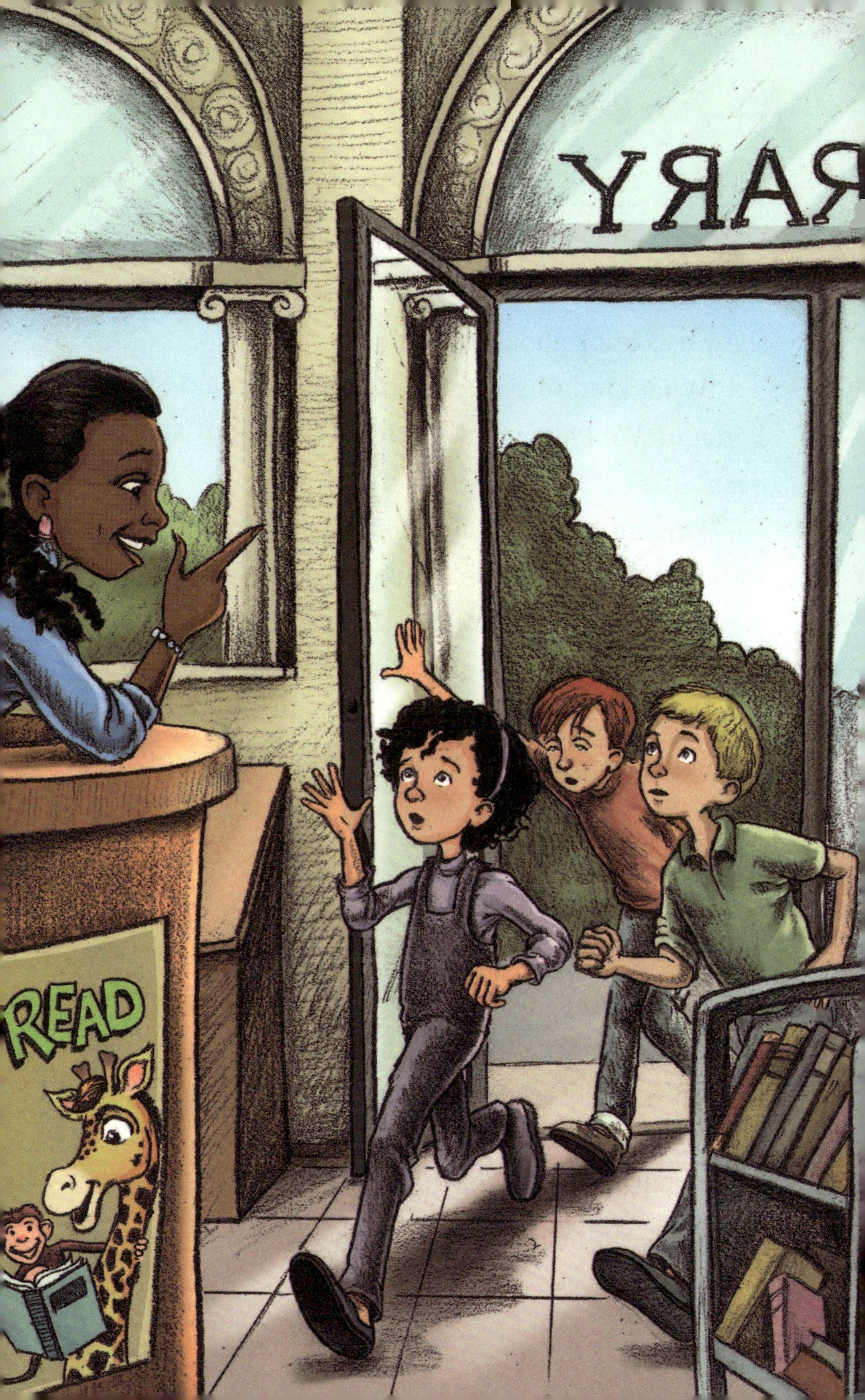
READ

faces are red as beets!"

"Hi, Mrs. Mackleroy," Ruth Rose panted. "Can you show us a book about stamps?"

"What kind of stamps, Ruth Rose? United States? Foreign? We have many, many books about stamps, dear."

"Do you have one about stamps with pictures of upside-down airplanes?" Dink asked.

Mrs. Mackleroy smiled. "You mean inverts," she said. "Stamps that were printed upside down by mistake."

She walked to a shelf and returned with a big flat book. "You should find your stamp in here," Mrs. Mackleroy said.

"Thanks a lot," Dink said.

Dink carried the book over to a corner table. He set it down, looked around, then pulled the envelopes from inside his shirt.

He carefully removed the blue stamp and placed it on the table.

"There's a zillion upside-down stamps in here," Josh said, riffling through the pages. "How do we find

一个空信封

ours?"

"Try the index," Dink said. "Under Jenny."

Josh turned to the index in the back of the book. He ran his finger down the J section. "No Jenny," he said.

"Try looking under airplanes," Ruth Rose suggested.

"Good idea!" Josh backed up a few pages to the A's. He found a listing for airplanes and turned to page 329.

And there it was. A picture of the little blue stamp.

Below the picture was a drawing of the airplane, only bigger. The caption read: CURTIS JENNY SINGLE-ENGINE AIRPLANE.

"Hey!" Josh said. "Jenny's the airplane!"

Silently the kids read the paragraph about the stamp.

"OH MY GOSH!" Ruth Rose yelled.

Mrs. Mackleroy tapped her pencil on the desk. "Ruth Rose, please," she said.

Dink picked up the little Jenny stamp. His fingers were shaking.

"This is worth fifty thousand dollars!" he whispered.

Chapter 6

"F-f-fifty thou...holy moly!" Josh squeaked.

The kids stared at the small blue stamp. After a minute, Dink slipped it back inside the envelope and put it in his pocket.

"No wonder Doris Duncan came all the way to Connecticut!" Ruth Rose said.

Dink nodded. "Yeah. She was after the stamp the whole time. I knew that story about her mother smelled fishy."

Josh closed the stamp book. "Well, we still have to give the stamp to her."

Dink and Ruth Rose looked at each other.

"Don't we?" Josh asked.

"I guess…" Dink said.

"What do you mean, 'I guess'?" Josh said. "It's hers, Dink. It was on her letter, no matter who sent it to her."

"But why was it hidden?" Dink asked. "Why the whole story about Doris's mother? Why the fake letters? Unless…"

"Unless what?" Josh asked.

Dink looked at Josh and Ruth Rose. "Unless the stamp is stolen…"

"Yes!" Ruth Rose said. "It's worth so much money! Maybe O. Bird stole it. Then he—or she—had to find a way to get it to Doris, so they thought up the letters from 'Mother.'"

Josh just looked at them. "You guys are crazy," he finally said. "Besides, there's no way to be sure."

Ruth Rose jumped up. "O. Bird sent the letters from New York, right? Maybe that's where the stamp was stolen!"

Ruth Rose hurried over to Mrs. Mackleroy's desk, spoke to her quickly, then came back.

"What's going on?" Dink asked.

"Mrs. Mackleroy is getting us the last few weeks' *New York Times*," Ruth Rose said. "We can check to see if there's anything about a missing stamp."

Dink looked at the clock. "Five-fifteen. Doris Duncan will be at my house in forty-five minutes!"

Mrs. Mackleroy walked over and dumped a pile of *New York Timeses* on their table. "Here you are, kids. Good luck!"

Josh stared at the mountain of papers. "Geez, it'll

take us all night to read these!"

"We don't have all night," Dink said, reaching for the pile. "Start reading!"

The kids each took a stack. They set aside the sections they didn't want, like sports, real estate, and entertainment.

For almost half an hour they turned pages.

The clock above Mrs. Mackleroy's desk ticked the minutes away.

"My eyes are getting blurry," Josh said. "There sure is a lot of stolen stuff in New York! Some guy even stole a chimpanzee from the zoo!"

Dink's back was hurting from bending over the table. His head ached, too, and his fingers were smudged gray from ink.

And then he found it.

"Here it is!" Dink said. He pointed to a headline and read:

SENIOR CITIZEN FINDS, THEN LOSES, FORTUNE

JUNE 20. Miss Clementine Painter, 73, was rich for a short time, but now she's poor again. While emptying her vacuum cleaner, she found a rare stamp among the dust. The stamp, worth more than $50,000, was later stolen from her room. New York City police are investigating.

Josh gulped. "You were right, Dink," he whispered. "You can't give the stamp to Doris Duncan!"

Mrs. Mackleroy approached their table. "I have to close up soon," she said.

Dink whipped his head around to look at the clock. Five-forty-eight! "Guys, we have twelve minutes before Doris Duncan comes back to my house!"

The kids thanked Mrs. Mackleroy, stacked the newspapers, and hurried out of the library.

On the library steps, Dink said, "Maybe we should tell Officer Fallon about Doris Duncan."

"But we still can't prove she did anything wrong,"

Josh said.

"Josh is right, Dink," Ruth Rose said. "Doris Duncan never got the letters or the stamp. If you tell Officer Fallon that she and O. Bird stole it, they'll say, 'Prove it!' "

"But what am I gonna do?" Dink asked. "It's almost six o'clock! I have to tell Doris Duncan something!"

The kids began walking toward Woody Street.

"I have an idea!" Ruth Rose said. "Why don't we glue the sunflower stamps back on the empty envelope, then hand over all five letters to Doris Duncan? She'll probably take them to her hotel room to read. Then we can run back here, give the Jenny stamp to Officer Fallon, and tell him the whole story."

"But how does that prove she's guilty?" Dink asked.

"Because then she'll have the letters!" Josh said.

Ruth Rose nodded. "And when Officer Fallon gets the letters from Doris and reads the hidden message, he'll know she and O. Bird stole the stamp."

Dink grinned. "Right. Then we can show him

一个空信封

what we just found in the newspaper. Okay, let's go!"

As they hurried down the library steps, Dink saw a dark car pull away from the curb.

"Hey, Josh, isn't that the same car you saw parked on my street?" he asked.

"Yeah, and the same weird-looking guy is driving!" Josh said.

"Josh, there wasn't anyone in that car," Ruth Rose said.

"Maybe he ducked down when you looked," Josh said. "But I know I saw someone in the driver's seat!"

"Whoever it is, we have to get going," Dink said. "It's nearly six o'clock!"

The kids ran up Main Street.

They took a shortcut through Center Park, then raced past the rose garden.

They were out of breath by the time they reached Woody Street.

A few houses away from Dink's, Josh suddenly grabbed Dink and Ruth Rose. He yanked them down behind Miss Alubicky's front hedge.

"What's wrong?" Dink asked.

127

"That same car is parked in front of your house again!" Josh said.

The kids peered over the hedge. A man and a woman got out of the car. Dink recognized Doris Duncan. The man was short and dressed in a green suit and purple tie.

"That's him!" Josh whispered. "The guy I saw in the car before!"

The kids watched Doris and the man talk for a few minutes, then get back into the car. But the car didn't drive away.

"What the heck are they doing?" Josh asked.

Dink gulped. He put his hand over the envelope holding the $50,000 stamp.

"They're waiting for me," he said.

Chapter 7

"What're we gonna do?" Ruth Rose asked. "That guy looks mean!"

"Maybe we should just give them the letters," Josh said.

"We can't!" Dink said. "The three sunflower stamps are still in Ruth Rose's house. They'll know we found the stolen stamp!"

"And we can't go home," Ruth Rose said. "They might grab us. Then they'd search us, and they'd find the stamp on Dink."

"Let's cut through the backyards to my house,"

Josh said. "We can call Officer Fallon and tell him we're being followed!"

"Okay," Dink said. "We can't just stay here."

The kids crawled across Miss Alubicky's lawn on their hands and knees. Suddenly her dog started barking at them.

一个空信封

Dink glanced back at the car. The driver's door flew open. The man in the green suit climbed out of the car and hollered at the kids.

"Let's go!" Josh yelled. They jumped up and raced through Miss Alubicky's backyard.

The man shot after them, crashing through Miss Alubicky's hedge.

"He's coming after us!" Dink cried. "Faster!"

A to Z 神秘案件

The kids tore across Eagle Lane and cut into the woods. They hid in some thick bushes to catch their breath.

The man stopped at the edge of the woods. The kids watched as he bent over, catching his breath.

一个空信封

"Come on!" Josh whispered. The minute they started running again, the man plunged into the trees after them.

They were faster than the man. A minute later, they raced through Josh's yard.

"Run into the barn and climb up to the loft!" Josh yelled.

"But we'll be trapped up there!" Dink said.

"Just do it!" Josh said. "I have an idea!"

The three kids sprinted into the barn. Dink and Ruth Rose scrambled up Josh's rope ladder into the loft.

Below him, Dink watched Josh shove open the rear door of the barn. But instead of running outside, Josh dove into a pile of hay.

Dink couldn't believe his eyes! "He's staying down there!" he said to Ruth Rose.

"Quick! Get the ladder!" Ruth Rose whispered.

Dink grabbed the ladder and pulled it into the loft.

Seconds later, the man in the green suit barreled through the barn door. Up in the loft, Dink could hear him gasping.

The man looked around the dim barn, then raced out the open rear door.

Dink almost laughed with relief. He started to get up. Suddenly Ruth Rose yanked him back down.

The man ran back into the barn. He stood in the middle and swiveled his head around like a snake.

Dink and Ruth Rose froze and carefully peered over the edge of the loft.

After a minute, the man kicked a pail across the

一个空信封

floor and stomped out of the barn.

Dink swallowed and let himself breathe again. He closed his eyes until he heard Josh whisper, "He's gone," from the hay pile.

Dink looked down and saw Josh's head pop up. With hay stuck in his red hair, he looked like a scarecrow.

Dink lowered the rope ladder. He and Ruth Rose climbed down. His legs felt like rubber.

They flopped down in the hay next to Josh. "What should we do?" Dink asked. "That jerk will just go back and sit outside my house."

The kids sat in the cool barn and thought. Then Ruth Rose sat up straight.

"I think I know how we can prove Doris Duncan and O. Bird stole the stamp," she said. "If I'm right, Officer Fallon will arrest them at the same time!"

"How?" Dink and Josh both said.

"I need a telephone," she said. "Can we go in your house, Josh?"

Josh crawled out of the hay and peeked out the barn door. "I don't see anyone," he said.

He quietly opened the door. The kids raced across his backyard and into the kitchen.

"What's your plan?" Dink asked Ruth Rose.

She told him.

Josh threw his arms into the air. "That is so excellent!" he cried.

Dink's eyes got big, then he grinned. "It's perfect! If it works, the stamp goes back where it belongs and those two crooks go to jail!"

Ruth Rose's first call was to Officer Fallon.

The boys listened as she explained about the letters, the stolen stamp, and her plan.

Ruth Rose listened, then started nodding. "Uh-huh. Got it. Right. Okay, bye!"

"What'd he say?" Dink asked.

Ruth Rose gave Dink a thumbs-up. Then she called information and got the number for the Shangri-la Hotel.

She dialed, then asked, "Is Doris Duncan there, please?"

Ruth Rose grinned at Dink and Josh. She mouthed the words. "They just walked in!"

一个空信封

When Ruth Rose started talking, she used a tough-guy voice.

Dink and Josh listened with their mouths open.

"Hello, Ms. Duncan? My name is Ruth Rose. I'm a friend of Dink's, and I got those letters you want!"

Ruth Rose made a gaggy face at the boys, then continued. "I got yer stamp, too. The one of the upside-down airplane."

She lowered her voice into a deep whisper. "And I know it's worth a lot of dough!"

Ruth Rose listened, then continued. "Dink is so dumb, he didn't know it was valuable. I'll sell it to you for five hundred bucks."

Dink and Josh broke into wide grins. Dink had to stop himself from laughing out loud.

Ruth Rose made a shushing motion with her free hand. "No, not tonight. I gotta go to my grandmother's. I'll meet you in the library tomorrow at high noon!"

Josh nearly fell on the floor laughing.

"Don't worry," Ruth Rose said. "I'll have the stamp. You just bring the five hundred smackers!"

137

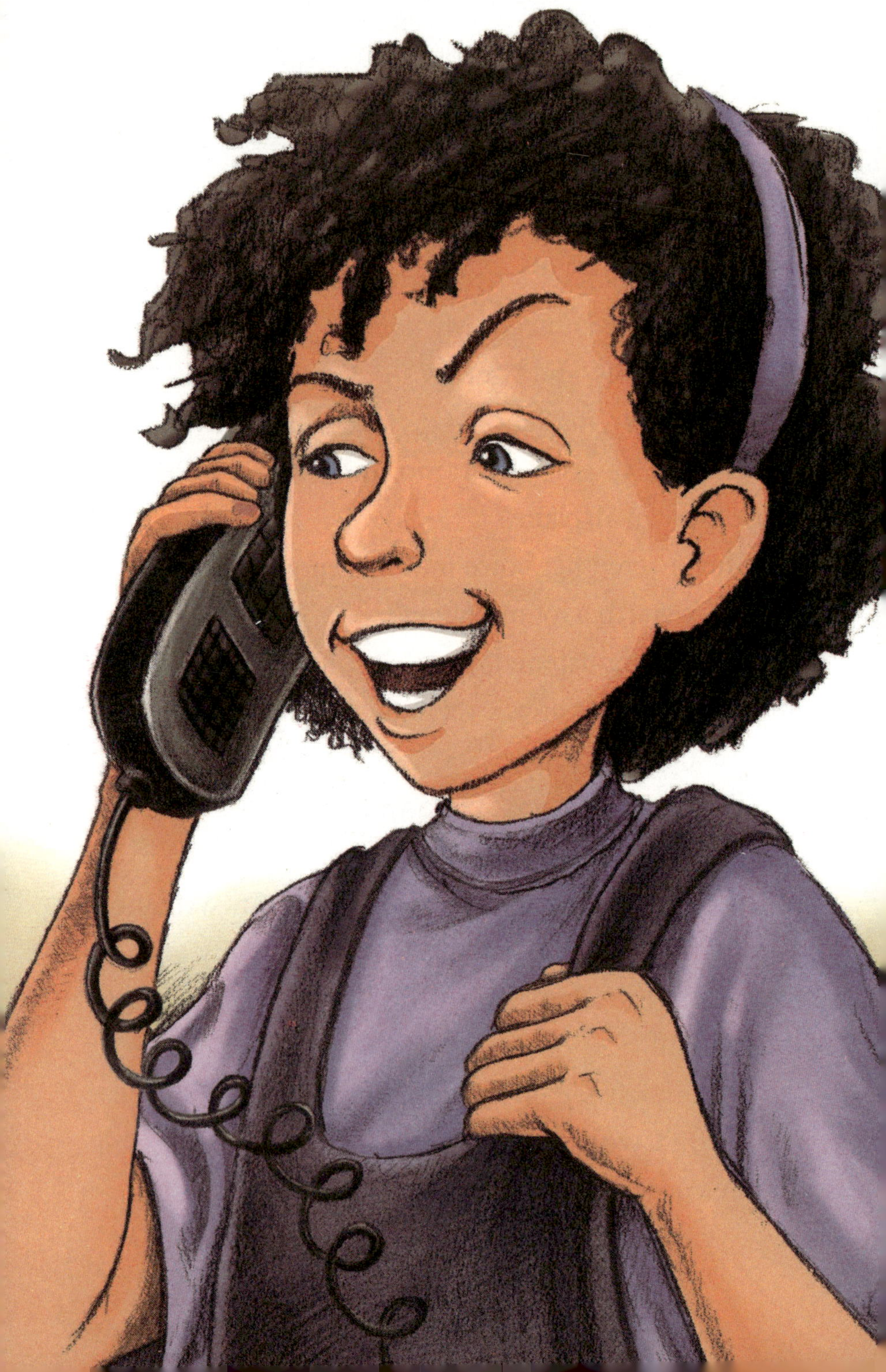

一个空信封

Then she hung up.

"Ruth Rose!" Josh yelled. "You sounded like a real crook! How did you do it?"

She smiled. "You ain't seen nothin' yet!"

Chapter 8

At noon the next day, Dink and Josh peeked out of Mrs. Mackleroy's office. Ruth Rose was sitting at a table, reading a book.

The library was nearly empty. An old woman sat reading a newspaper. A man was snoozing near the door with his cap pulled over his eyes. Mrs. Mackleroy was on her lunch break.

"Ruth Rose looks so calm," Dink whispered. "I feel like I'm gonna be sick!"

"If you throw up, I'll kill you," Josh said. He grinned. "And Mrs. Mackleroy will rip up your library

一个空信封

card!"

A minute later, Doris Duncan walked into the library. The man in the green suit followed her. He had long, strong-looking arms and a thick neck.

Dink shuddered. It was the man who had chased them! He nudged Josh as the two walked across the room.

"Are you Ruth Rose?" Dink heard Doris Duncan ask.

Ruth Rose nodded.

She held up the five blue envelopes. "The stamp is inhere," she said, showing Doris Duncan the empty one.

"I hope Ruth Rose gets the money first," Josh whispered.

Ruth Rose looked at the man and raised her eyebrows. "Who's he?" she asked in her bad-guy voice.

"This is my associate," Doris Duncan said. "Mr. Otto Bird."

"Aha!" said Dink in the office.

"Did you bring the cash?" asked Ruth Rose.

The woman snapped her fingers. Otto Bird yanked

some bills from his pocket and handed them to Doris Duncan.

"Lemme see da stamp foist," he croaked.

Josh started to giggle. Dink clapped a hand over his mouth.

Ruth Rose slid the stamp out of the envelope.

"See, there's the upside-down airplane," Dink heard her say.

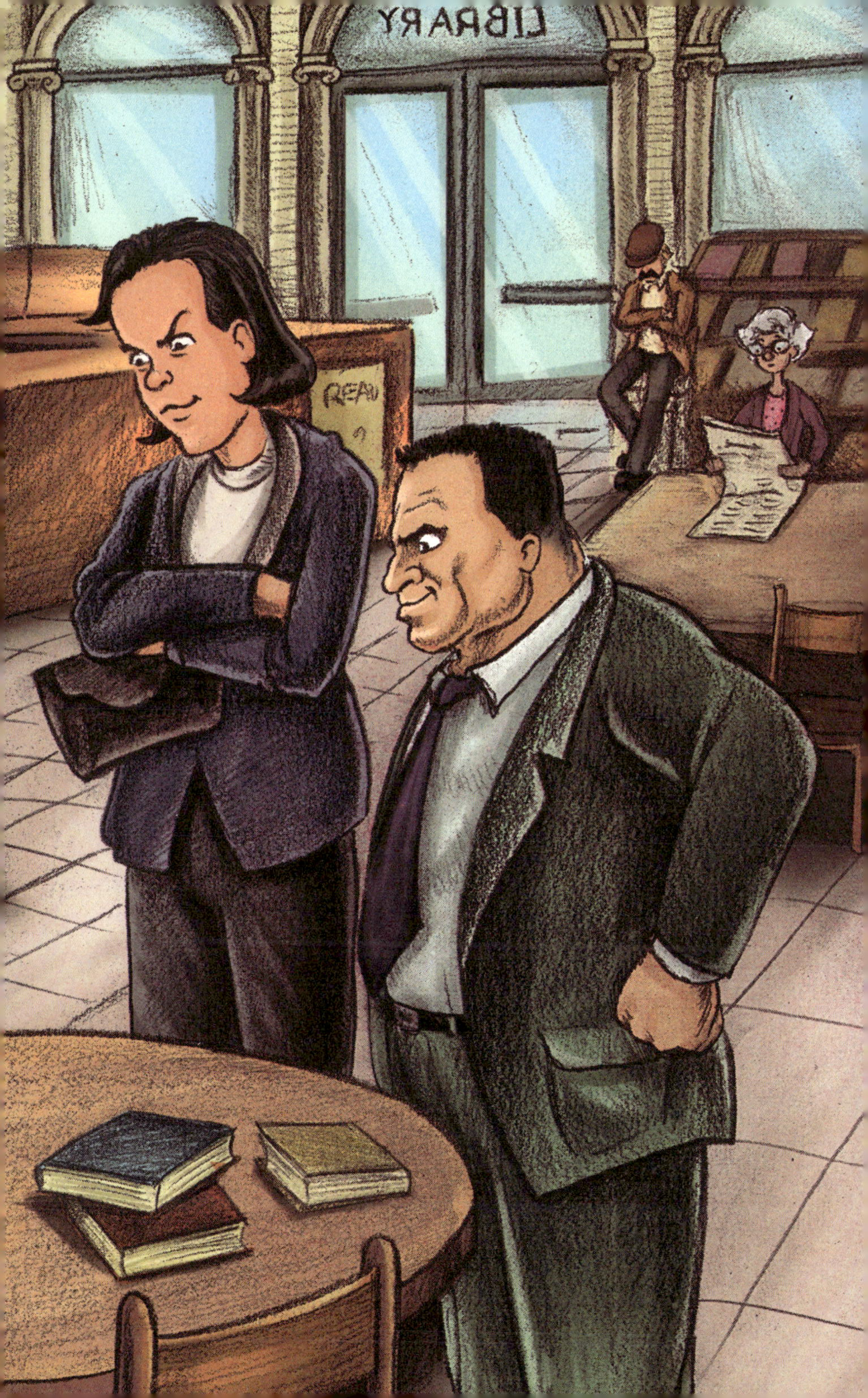
LIBRARY

Otto Bird snatched the stamp out of Ruth Rose's fingers. With his other hand, he whipped out a magnifying glass.

The man examined the stamp through bulging eyes. Then he smirked. "Dis is da one," he said.

Ruth Rose smiled sweetly. "The money, please," she said.

Doris Duncan dropped five one-hundred-dollar bills into Ruth Rose's hand.

In the office, Dink and Josh high-fived.

Ruth Rose counted the money. Out loud. When she finished, she looked at Doris Duncan and Otto Bird.

Then she hollered, "OKAY, OFFICER FALLON!"

The man snoozing by the door stood up.

"Don't move, you two!" Officer Fallon said. "You're under arrest for theft and mail fraud!"

Chapter 9

Officer Fallon snapped handcuffs on the thieves' wrists.

"I'll take that," he said, plucking the Jenny stamp from Otto's hand.

Doris Duncan shot Ruth Rose a nasty look. "You tricked us!" she screamed.

The old woman who had been reading a newspaper suddenly stood up. She had white hair and wore a neat dress covered with tiny pink flowers.

The woman folded the paper and placed it on the table. Then she crossed the room.

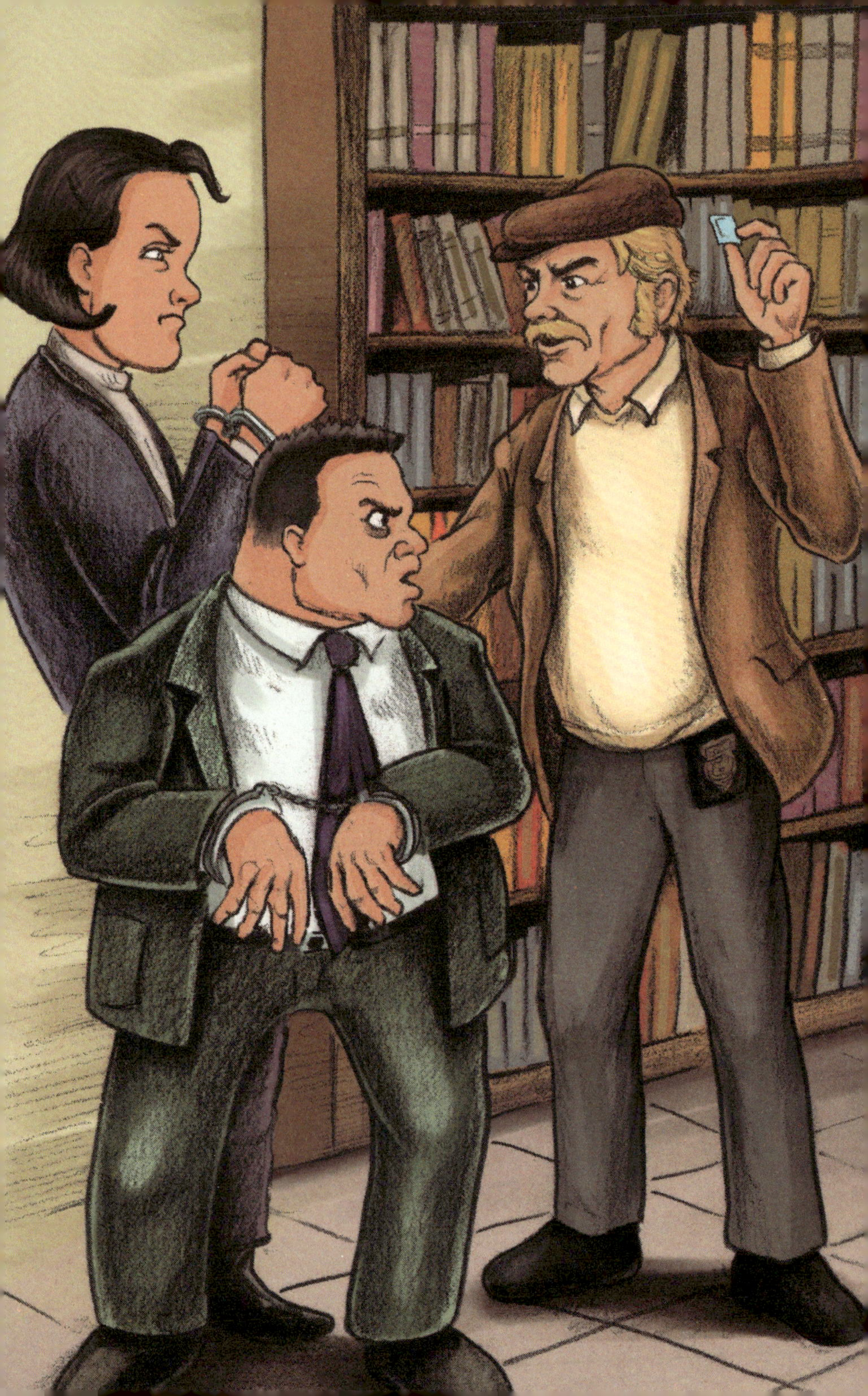

"No, you tricked me!" the woman said. She turned to Otto Bird. "Remember me—Clementine Painter? You lied to me. You told me you were a stamp expert, but you're nothing but a crook!"

When Otto Bird recognized Clementine Painter, his mouth dropped open. Not a word came out.

In the office, Dink and Josh danced around Mrs. Mackleroy's desk. "Gotcha!" Dink shouted.

The day before, when Ruth Rose had telephoned Officer Fallon, he told her he'd call Clementine Painter. With her there, Officer Fallon had explained,

Doris Duncan and Otto Bird wouldn't stand a chance.

Clementine had hopped on a bus for Green Lawn to get her stamp back.

When Dink and Josh walked out of the office, Doris Duncan's squinty eyes got big. Then they closed, as if she had a bad headache.

Otto Bird's face turned as purple as his tie. Dink thought the man would explode.

"You can't prove nothin'!" Otto Bird yelled. He raised his cuffed hands and pointed at Doris. "She planned the whole thi—"

"Shut up, frog-face!" Doris Duncan snapped at Otto Bird. "If you'd copied down the right zip code, we wouldn't be in this two-bit town to begin with!"

Office Fallon chuckled. "Don't worry, you won't be in two-bit Green Lawn for long. I hear New York has a million-dollar jail!"

Officer Fallon led the stamp thieves to the door. "I'll meet you folks at Ellie's Diner in an hour," he said over his shoulder.

The kids and Clementine hurried to the window. They saw Officer Fallon lead the two thieves across

一个空信封

the street and into the police station.

"My soul," Clementine said to the kids. "That was so exciting. Better than television!"

An hour later, they all met inside Ellie's Diner. Clementine treated the kids to ice cream.

"It feels lovely to be able to buy things for people," she said. "I thought I'd lost that stamp forever."

"How did it get in your vacuum cleaner?" asked Dink.

Clementine smiled, but it was a sad smile. "My mother died recently. She was ninety-six. I was cleaning out her old vacuum cleaner when I found the stamp. She must have vacuumed it up, but who knows when or where?"

"How did you know it was valuable?" Ruth Rose asked.

"I didn't!" Clementine said. "But I knew it was old, so I looked up a stamp organization in the phone book." She shook her head. "And that's when all the trouble started!"

Officer Fallon nodded. "Otto sang like a bird,"

149

he said. "Seems he worked for the stamp outfit you called. When you telephoned to ask about your stamp, he answered the phone."

"He was ever so polite," Clementine said. "He told me to hide the stamp, and he'd come right over to look at it."

Clementine looked angry. "He asked to see the stamp. Like an old fool, I showed him my hiding place."

"Where?" Josh asked.

Clementine blushed. "In my cookie jar," she said. "I treat myself to one cookie every day with my tea!"

Dink laughed. "That stamp has been everywhere!"

"I don't understand how it got under those other stamps," Clementine said.

"Otto Bird hid it under regular stamps so he could mail it to Doris Duncan's home in Colorado," Officer Fallon explained. "They planned to sell the stamp, then split the fifty thousand dollars."

"But why did Otto Bird write those letters?" Dink asked.

"They both have records with the police," Officer

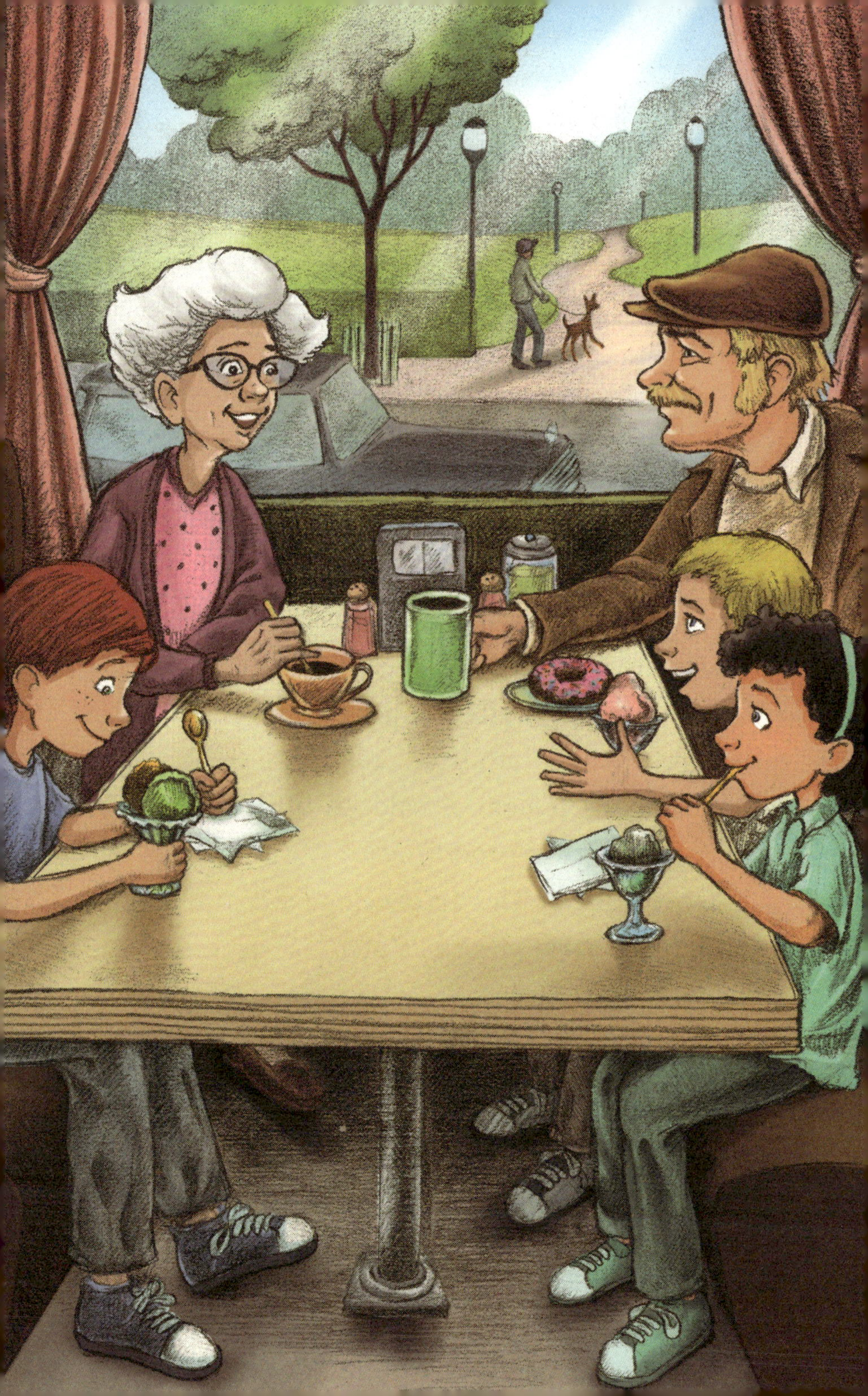

Fallon said. "In case anyone opened the envelopes, they had to look innocent. That's why he signed them 'Mother'."

"And when Doris Duncan got the notes, she'd know where to find the stamp," Ruth Rose said.

"But she didn't get them!" Josh said.

Officer Fallon smiled. "Right. Lucky for Miss Painter, Otto broke his glasses and copied down the zip code for Green Lawn, Connecticut, instead of Green Lawn, Colorado."

"And then my little brother hid the envelopes in the refrigerator!" Ruth Rose added.

"Mercy!" Clementine said. "All this commotion over a tiny piece of paper!"

Officer Fallon slid an envelope across the table. "Here's your stamp, Miss Painter." He grinned. "Can you find a safer hiding place?"

"You bet, sir!" she said. "This is going right into the bank!"

Everyone said good-bye, and Officer Fallon took Clementine back to the bus station.

The kids walked home, talking about finding a

一个空信封

fortune in a vacuum cleaner.

"Want to come over and play more volleyball?" Dink asked.

"Sure. Nate and I were winning!" Ruth Rose said.

Josh grinned. "Not me. I'm going right home. I want to see what's inside my mom's vacuum cleaner!"

Text copyright © 1998 by Ron Roy
Cover art copyright © 2015 by Stephen Gilpin
Interior illustrations copyright © 1998 by John Steven Gurney
All rights reserved. Published in the United States by Random House Children's Books,
a division of Random House LLC, a Penguin Random House Company, New York.
Originally published in paperback by Random House Children's Books, New York, in 1998.

本书中英双语版由中南博集天卷文化传媒有限公司与企鹅兰登（北京）文化发展有限公司合作出版。

"企鹅"及其相关标识是企鹅兰登已经注册或尚未注册的商标。
未经允许，不得擅用。
封底凡无企鹅防伪标识者均属未经授权之非法版本。

©中南博集天卷文化传媒有限公司。本书版权受法律保护。未经权利人许可，任何人不得以任何方式使用本书包括正文、插图、封面、版式等任何部分内容，违者将受到法律制裁。

著作权合同登记号：字18-2023-258

图书在版编目（CIP）数据

一个空信封：汉英对照／（美）罗恩·罗伊著；
（美）约翰·史蒂文·格尼绘；杨琼琼译. -- 长沙：湖
南少年儿童出版社，2024.10. --（A to Z神秘案件）.
ISBN 978-7-5562-7817-6

Ⅰ．H319.4

中国国家版本馆CIP数据核字第2024W80X33号

A TO Z SHENMI ANJIAN YI GE KONG XINFENG
A to Z神秘案件 一个空信封

[美] 罗恩·罗伊 著　　[美] 约翰·史蒂文·格尼 绘　　杨琼琼 译

责任编辑：唐凌　李炜	策划出品：李炜　张苗苗　文赛峰
策划编辑：文赛峰	特约编辑：张晓璐
营销编辑：付佳　杨朔　周晓茜	封面设计：霍雨佳
版权支持：王媛媛	版式设计：马睿君
插图上色：河北传图文化	内文排版：马睿君

出　版　人：刘星保
出　　　版：湖南少年儿童出版社
地　　　址：湖南省长沙市晚报大道89号
邮　　　编：410016
电　　　话：0731-82196320
常年法律顾问：湖南崇民律师事务所　柳成柱律师
经　　　销：新华书店
开　　　本：875 mm × 1230 mm　1/32
字　　　数：85千字
版　　　次：2024年10月第1版
书　　　号：ISBN 978-7-5562-7817-6
印　　　刷：三河市中晟雅豪印务有限公司
印　　　张：4.875
次：2024年10月第1次印刷
定　　　价：280.00元（全10册）

若有质量问题，请致电质量监督电话：010-59096394　团购电话：010-59320018